Bayard Taylor

The Echo Club : and other Literary Diversions

Bayard Taylor

The Echo Club : and other Literary Diversions

ISBN/EAN: 9783743308220

Manufactured in Europe, USA, Canada, Australia, Japa

Cover: Foto ©ninafisch / pixelio.de

Manufactured and distributed by brebook publishing software (www.brebook.com)

Bayard Taylor

The Echo Club : and other Literary Diversions

THE ECHO CLUB,

And Other Literary Diversions.

BY

BAYARD TAYLOR.

BOSTON:
JAMES R. OSGOOD AND COMPANY,
Late Ticknor & Fields, and Fields, Osgood, & Co.
1876.

Copyright, 1872 and 1876.
By JAMES R. OSGOOD & CO.

University Press: Welch, Bigelow, & Co.,
Cambridge.

CONTENTS.

	PAGE
INTRODUCTION	v

NIGHT THE FIRST. 11
    MORRIS, POE, BROWNING.

NIGHT THE SECOND 34
    MRS. SIGOURNEY, KEATS, SWINBURNE, EMERSON, STEDMAN.

NIGHT THE THIRD 52
    BARRY CORNWALL, WHITTIER, ROSSETTI, ALDRICH.

NIGHT THE FOURTH 72
    BRYANT, HOLMES, WILLIS, TENNYSON.

NIGHT THE FIFTH 93
    TUCKERMAN, LONGFELLOW, STODDARD, MRS. STODDARD.

NIGHT THE SIXTH 113
    LOWELL, BAYARD TAYLOR, MRS. BROWNING, BOKER.

NIGHT THE SEVENTH 132
    JEAN INGELOW, BUCHANAN READ, JULIA WARD HOWE, PIATT, WILLIAM WINTER, MRS. PIATT.

CONTENTS.

NIGHT THE EIGHTH 150
    WALT WHITMAN, BRET HARTE, JOHN HAY, JOAQUIN MILLER.

THE BATTLE OF THE BARDS 168

A REVIEW 175

PARADISE DISCOVERED 186

INTRODUCTION.

THE papers which make up this volume are sufficiently described by its title. They are literary "Diversions,"— the product of a good many random hours of thoughtless (or, at least, only half-thoughtful) recreation and amusement,— nothing else. More than as many burlesque imitations of authors, living or dead, as are here contained, had been written before any thought of publication was suggested. The fact that there was no such original design requires that the form in which the diversions are now presented should be explained to the reader.

The habit originated, very much as it is described in the "First Evening," at least twenty years ago, in a small private circle. Three or four young authors found not only amusement, but an agreeable relaxation from their graver tasks, in drawing names and also subjects as from a lottery-wheel, and improvising imitations of older and more renowned poets. Nothing was further from their minds than ridicule, or even incidental disparagement, of the latter, many of whom were not only recognized, but genuinely revered, by all. One form of intellectual diversion gradually led to another: the parodies alternated with the filling up of end-rhymes (usually of the most difficult and incongruous character), with the writing of double or concealed acrostics, spurious quotations from various languages, and whatever else could be devised by the ingenuity of the company. I may mention that some years before Mr. Lewis Carroll delighted all lovers of nonsense with his ballad of "The Jabberwock," we tried precisely the same experiment of introducing invented words. The following four lines may serve as a specimen of one attempt:—

> "Smitten by harsh, transcetic thuds of shame,
> My squelgence fades: I mogrify my blame:
> The lupkin world, that leaves me yole and blant,
> Denies my affligance with looks askant!"

Of course, nothing further than amusing nonsense was ever contemplated. A few of the imitations found their way into print, but they were comparatively unnoticed in the flood of burlesque with which the public was then supplied from many other quarters. As a participant, for several years, in a variety of fun which was certainly harmless so long as it remained private, I was of the opinion that very little could be made public without some accompanying explanation. The idea of setting the imitations in a framework of dialogue which should represent various forms of literary taste and opinion seemed, first, to make the publication possible. But when I came to examine the scattered leaves with a view to this end, I was at once struck with their inadequacy to the purpose of comical illustration. Removed from the genial atmosphere in which they had spontaneously grown, many of them seemed withered and insipid. Many others were simply parodies of particular poems, instead of being burlesque reproductions of an author's manner and diction. The plan demanded that they should be rewritten, in consonance with the governing conception of the work, as a whole. This was accordingly done; and not more than three or four of the following poems belong to the original private "diversions."

There is scarcely a more hazardous experiment which an author can make, than to attempt to draw amusement from the intellectual characteristics of his contemporaries. If I had not been firmly convinced that the absence of any conscious unfriendliness on my part *must* make itself evident to many who were old and honored friends, I never should have dared it. In addition to this, I ventured on a number of private tests, and was further assured by finding that the subject of each travesty accepted his share with the greatest good-nature. I have yet to learn that the publication has given other than a very slight momentary annoyance, and that only in one or two cases. It is doubtful whether the same experiment could be made in any of the other arts, with a similar result. I am satisfied that opera-singers, actors, composers, sculptors, painters, theologians even, have a better right to be called the *genus irritabile* than the literary guild. The more devotedly an author aspires towards his ideal of achievement, the less he is concerned with all transitory estimates of his work. Looking back now, four years since the papers appeared in the "Atlantic Monthly," I see more clearly how much was ventured, and I am profoundly grateful to find that no serious wound was given.

Some of my friends have suggested that the characters introduced in the Echo Club, and the course of their dialogues, might have been made more interesting to the reader. This is probably true; but, on the other hand, all work of the kind has but an ephemeral interest, and the leisure of mind which produced it seems now so remote, so beyond recall, that I have not undertaken to make any change. The four principal characters were designed to represent classes, not individuals. In "The Ancient," I endeavored to express something of the calmer judicial temper, in literary matters, which comes from age and liberal study. The name of "Zoïlus" (the *Homeromastix*, or "Scourge of Homer") explains his place: he is the carping, cynical, unconsciously arrogant critic, — though these qualities could not be given with entire dramatic truth. "Galahad" is the young, sensational, impressive element in the reading public; admiration, in him, is almost equivalent to adoration. "The Gannet" — a name suggested by a poem written by a member of the class, long ago — represents brilliancy without literary principle, the love of technical effect, regardless of the intellectual conception of a work. This is a class which is always large, and always more or less successful — for a time. It was not necessary that each character should keep rigidly within the limits of his part, and thus each of them may be occasionally inconsistent. I need hardly explain that the author's own views, though scattered here and there through the dialogues, together with their exact opposites, are not specially expressed by any one of the four persons.

The papers were meant to be anonymous, but the secret was soon betrayed, — not, however, before some amusing illustrations of the personal character of much so-called criticism were furnished. The comments of certain writers for the press, before and after the authorship was known, formed a curious and instructive contrast. In London, the papers were collected and published as a volume, more than two years ago; and there may be possibly enough diversion still lingering about them to satisfy the indolent mood of a summer afternoon. More than this is not intended by their appearance in the present form.

I have added some other specimens of the same kind of fooling, partly in order to put everything of the sort in its place and leave it behind me, and partly because a good many personal friends have been amused, and hence some unknown friends may also be. This prelude is no doubt longer than necessary; but on completing and offering to others a diversion which will never be repeated, one may be pardoned for an over-scrupulousness in explaining circumstances and justifying motives.

B. T.

NEW YORK, June, 1876.

Diversions of the Echo Club.

NIGHT THE FIRST.

IF it were not that the public cherishes rather singular and fluctuating notions with regard to the private and familiar intercourse of authors, the reports which follow would need no prologue. But between the two classes of readers, one of which innocently supposes T. Percy Jones to be the strange and terrible being whom they find represented in his "Firmilian," while the other, having discovered, by a few startling disillusions, that the race of authors is Janus-faced, is sure that T. Percy Jones is the exact opposite of his poetical self, there has arisen a confusion which it may be well to correct.

The authors themselves, I am aware, are chiefly responsible for these opposite impressions. When Joaquin Miller at Niagara, standing on the brink of the American precipice, kisses his hands grandly to Canada, exclaiming, "England, I thank you!" or when Martin Farquhar Tupper, in a speech at New York, cries out with noble magnanimity, "America, be not afraid, *I* will protect you!" the public might reasonably expect to find all poets visibly trailing their mantles in our streets. But when an eager listener, stealing behind Irving and Halleck at an evening party, found them talking of — shoe-leather! and a breathless devotee of Thackeray, sitting opposite to him at the dinner-table, saw those Delphian lips unclose only to utter the words, "Another potato, if you please!" — they had revelations which might cast a dreadful suspicion over the nature of the whole tribe of authors.

I would not have the reader imagine that the members of the Echo Club are represented by either of these extremes. They are authors, of different ages and very unequal places in public estimation. It would never occur to them to seat themselves on self-constructed pyramids, and speak as if The Ages were listening; yet, like their brethren of all lands and all times, the staple of their talk is literature. What Englishmen call "the shop," is an inevitable feature of their conversation. They can never come together without discussing the literary news of the day, the qualities of prominent authors, living or dead, and sometimes their own. However the enlightened listener might smile at the positiveness of their opinions, and the contradictions into which they are sometimes led in the lawless play and keen clash of the lighter intellect, he could not fail to recognize the sovereign importance they attach to their art. Without lifting from their intercourse that last veil of mystery, behind which only equals are permitted to pass, I may safely try to report the mixture of sport and earnest, of satire and enthusiasm, of irreverent audacity and pure aspiration, which met and mingled at their meetings. If the reader cannot immediately separate these elements, it is no fault of mine. He is most desirous, I know, to be present at the private diversions of a small society of authors, and to hear them talk as they are wont to talk when the wise heads of the world are out of ear-shot.

The character which the society assumed for a short time was entirely accidental. As one of the Chorus, I was present at the first meeting, and of course I never failed afterwards. The four authors who furnished our entertainment were not aware that I had written down, from memory, the substance of the conversations, until our evenings came to an end; and I have had some difficulty in obtaining their permission to publish my reports. The Ancient and Galahad feared that certain poets whom they delight to honor might be annoyed, not so much at the sportive imitation of their manner, as at the possible misconception of its purpose by the public. But Zoïlus and the Gannet agreed with me, that where no harm is meant none can be inflicted; that the literature of our day is in a sad state of bewilderment and confusion, and that a few effervescing powders would perhaps soothe a public stomach which has been overdosed with startling effects.

At last the Ancient said: "So be it, then! Take the poems, but don't bring your manuscript to us for correction! I am quite sure you have often reported us falsely, and if our masks of names are pulled off, we will have that defence."

I have only to add that the three or four gentlemen

comprising the Chorus are not authors by profession. The Ancient is in the habit of dividing the race of artists into active and passive, — the latter possessing the artistic temperament, the tastes, the delights, the instincts of the race, — everything, except that creative gadfly which stings to expression. In every quality except production they are the equals of the producers, he says; and they are quite as necessary to the world as the active artists, since they are the first to recognize the good points of the latter, to strengthen them with warm and intelligent sympathy, and to commend them to the slower perceptions and more uncertain tastes of the mass of readers. I am sure, at least, that our presence and participation in the amusements was a gentle stimulus to the principal actors. We were their enthusiastic audience, and kept them fresh and warm to their work. I do not record our share in the conversation, for there is sufficient diversity of opinion without it; and I made no notes of it at the time. — THE NAMELESS REPORTER.

In the rear of Karl Schäfer's lager-beer cellar and restaurant — which every one knows is but a block from the central part of Broadway — there is a small room, with a vaulted ceiling, which Karl calls his *Löwengrube*, or Lions' Den. Here, in their Bohemian days, Zoïlus and the Gannet had been accustomed to meet to discuss literary projects, and read fragments of manuscript to each other. The Chorus, the Ancient, and young Galahad gradually fell into the same habit, and thus a little circle of six, seven, or eight members came to be formed. The room could comfortably contain no more: it was quiet, with a dim, smoky, confidential atmosphere, and suggested Auerbach's Cellar to the Ancient, who had been in Leipzig.

Here, authors, books, magazines, and newspapers were talked about; sometimes a manuscript poem was read by its writer; while mild potations of beer and the dreamy breath of cigars delayed the nervous, fidgety, clattering-footed American Hours. One night they chanced upon a discussion of Morris's "Earthly Paradise," which Galahad rapturously admired, while the Ancient continued to draw him out, at first by guarded praise, then by critical objections to the passages which Galahad quoted. The conversation finally took this turn: —

GALAHAD. Indeed, you are not just! Tell me, have you read the whole work?

THE ANCIENT. Yes: I had it with me on my last trip to Havana, and read all three volumes under the most favorable auspices, — lying on deck in the shadow of a sail, with the palms and mangroves of the Bahamas floating past, in the distance. Just so I floated through the narrative poems, one after the other, admiring the story-teller's art, heartily enjoying many passages, accepting even the unnecessary quaintness of the speech, and at first disposed to say, "Here is a genuine poet!" But I was conscious of a lack of something, which, in my lazy mood, I did not attempt to analyze. When the lines and scenes and characters began to fade in my mind (which they did almost immediately), I found that the final impression which the work left behind was very much like the Hades of the Greeks, — a gray, misty, cheerless land, full of wandering shadows, — a place, where there is no sun, no clear, conscious, joyous life, where even fortunate love is sad, where hope is unknown to the heart, and there is nothing in the distance but death, and nothing after death. There had been a languid and rather agreeable sense of enjoyment; but it was followed by a chill.

GALAHAD. Oh!

THE GANNET. How often have I told you, Galahad, that you 're too easily taken off your feet! He 's very clever, I admit; but there 's a deal of trick in it, for all that. His revival of obsolete words, his imitation of Chaucer —

GALAHAD (*impatiently*). Imitation!

THE GANNET. Well, — only half, and half similarity of talent. But no writer can naturally assume a manner of speech which has long fallen into disuse, even in literature: so far as he does so, he is artificial. And this artifice Morris carries into his pictures of sentiment and passion. You cease to feel with and for his characters, long before he has done with them.

GALAHAD. As human beings, perhaps; but as conceptions of beauty, they have another existence.

THE GANNET. When I want a Greek frieze, let me have it in marble! Yes, he 's a skilful workman, and a successful one, as his popularity proves. And he 's lucky in producing his canned fruit after Swinburne's curry and pepper-sauce: but it is *canned*. I don't say I could equal him in his own line, for that requires natural inclination as well as knack, yet I think I could give you something exactly in his style, in ten minutes.

THE ANCIENT. Challenge him, Galahad!

THE GANNET. Get me paper and pencil! I will at

least try. Now, Galahad, put up your watch; I only stipulate that you don't time me too exactly. Stay!— take another sheet and try the same thing yourself.

(*They write; meanwhile the others talk.*)

THE GANNET (*after twenty minutes*). I have failed in time, because I began wrong. I tried to write a serious passage in Morris's manner, and my own habit of expression immediately came in as a disturbing influence. Then I gave up the plan of producing something really earnest and coherent,— that is, I kept in mind the manner, alone, and let the matter come of itself. Very little effort was required, I found: the lines arranged themselves easily enough. Now, lend me your ears: it is a passage from "The Taming of Themistocles," in the ninth volume of the " Earthly Paradise": (*Reads.*)

" He must be holpen ; yet how help shall I,
Steeped to the lips in ancient misery,
And by the newer grief apparelléd ?
If that I throw these ashes on mine head,
Do this thing for thee, — while about my way
A shadow gathers, and the piteous day,
So wan and bleak for very loneliness,
Turneth from sight of such unruthfulness ? "
Therewith he caught an arrow from the sheaf,
And brake the shaft in witlessness of grief ;
But Chiton's vest, such dismal fear she had,
Shook from the heart that sorely was a-drad,
And she began, withouten any pause,
To say : " Why break the old Ætolian laws,
Send this man forth, that never harm hath done,
Between the risen and the setten sun ?"

B

And next, they wandered to a steepy hill,
Whence all the land was lying gray and still,
And not a living creature there might be,
From the cold mountains to the salt, cold sea;
Only, within a little cove, one sail
Shook, as it whimpered at the cruel gale,
And the mast moaned from chafing of the rope;
So all was pain: they saw not any hope.

ZOÏLUS. But that is no imitation! You have copied a passage out of — out of — pshaw! I know the poem, and I remember the lines.

THE GANNET (*indignantly*). Out of Milton, why not say? — where you'll be just as likely to find them. Now, let me hear yours, Galahad; you were writing.

GALAHAD (*crushing the paper in his hand*). Mine is neither one thing nor the other, — not the author's poetic dialect throughout, nor hinting of his choice of subjects. I began something, which was really my own, and then gradually ran into an echo. I think *you* have hit upon the true method; and we must try again, since we know it.

THE GANNET. Why not try others, — a dozen of them? By Jove, I should like some mere gymnastics, after the heavy prose I've been writing! And you, too, Galahad, and the Ancient (if his ponderous dignity does n't prevent it); and here's Zoïlus, the very fellow for such a diversion! We can come together, here, and be a private, secret club of Parodists, — of Echoes, — of Iconoclasts, — of —

THE ANCIENT. Of irreverent satirists, I fear. That would be a new kind of a *Hainbund*, indeed; but, after all, it need not be ill-natured. At least, to insure yourselves against relapsing into mere burlesque and incidental depreciation, — which is a tempting, but nearly always a fatal course, for young writers, — I must be present. My indifferentism, as you call it, which sometimes provokes you when I cannot share all your raptures, may do good service in keeping you from rushing into the opposite extreme. As for taking part in the work, I won't promise to do much. You know I am a man of uncertain impulses, and can get nothing out of myself by force of resolution.

OMNES. O, you must take part! It will be capital sport.

THE ANCIENT (*deliberately, between the whiffs of his cigar*). First of all, let us clearly understand what is to be done. To undertake *parodies*, as the word is generally comprehended, — that is, to make a close imitation of some particular poem, though it should be characteristic of the author, — would be rather a flat business. Even the Brothers Smith and Bon Gaultier, admirable as they are, stuck too closely to selected models; and Phebe Cary, who has written the best American parodies, did the same thing. I think the Gannet has discovered something altogether more original and satisfactory, — a simple echo of the author's tone and manner. The choice of a subject gives another chance of fun.

(*He takes up the* GANNET'S *imitation and looks over it.*)

Here the dialect and movement and atmosphere are suggested; the exaggeration is neither coarse nor extreme, and the comical effect seems to lie mainly in the circumstance that it *is* a wilful imitation. If we were to find the passage in one of Morris's poems, we might think it carelessly written, somewhat obscure, but still in the same key with what precedes and follows it. Possibly, nay, almost certainly, it would not amuse us at all; but just now I noticed that even Galahad could not help laughing. A diversion of this sort is less a labor and more a higher and finer recreation of the mind, than the mechanical setting of some given poem, line by line, to a ludicrous subject, like those endless and generally stupid parodies of Longfellow's "Excelsior" and Emerson's "Brahma." For heaven's — no, Homer's — sake, let us not fall into that vein!

The Gannet. Thou speakest well.

Galahad. But how shall we select the authors? And shall I be required to make my own demigods ridiculous?

Zoïlus. Let me prove to you, by one of your own demigods, that nothing can be either sublime or ridiculous. Poetry is the Brahma of literature, — above all, pervading all, self-existent, though so few find her (and men of business reckon ill who leave her out), and therefore quite unmoved by anything we may do. Don't you remember the lines? —

> "Far or forgot to me is near,
> Shadow and sunlight are the same;
> The vanished gods to me appear,
> And one to me are shame and fame."

The Ancient. You are right, Zoïlus, in spite of your sarcasm. Besides, it is an evidence of a poet's distinct individuality, when he can be amusingly imitated. We can only make those the objects of our fun whose manner or dialect stamps itself so deeply into our minds that a new cast can be taken. We are sporting around great, and sometimes little names, like birds or cats or lizards around the feet, and over the shoulders, and on the heads of statues. Now, there's an idea for a poem, Galahad. But, seriously, how would you imitate Pollok's "Course of Time," or Young's "Night Thoughts," or Blair's "Grave," or any other of those masses of words, which are too ponderous for poetry and too respectable for absurdity! Either extreme will do for us, excellence or imbecility; but it must have a distinct, pronounced character.

THE GANNET. Come, now! I'm eager for another trial.

THE ANCIENT. Let us each write the names of three or four poets on separate slips of paper, and throw them into my hat; then let each draw out one slip as his model for to-night. Thus there will be no clashing of tastes or inclinations, and our powers of imitation will be more fairly tested.

(*They write three names apiece, the* CHORUS *taking part. Then all are thrown into the* THE ANCIENT'S *hat and shaken up together.*)

GALAHAD (*drawing*). Robert Browning.

THE GANNET. So is mine.

ZOÏLUS. Edgar A. Poe.

THE ANCIENT. Some of us have written the same names. Well, let it be so to-night. If we find the experiment diverting, we can easily avoid any such repetition next time. Moreover, Browning alone will challenge echoes from all of us; and I am curious to see whether the several imitations will reflect the same characteristics of his style. It will, at least, show whether the stamp upon each mind has any common likeness to the original.

The Gannet. A good idea! But Zoïlus is already possessed by the spirit of Poe; not, I hope, in the manner of Dr. Garth Wilkinson of London, whose volume of poems dictated by the spirits of the dead authors is the most astonishing collection I ever saw. He makes Poe's "wet locks" rhyme to his "fetlocks"! It is even worse than Harris's "Epic of the Starry Heavens," dictated to him in forty-eight hours by Dante. By the by, we have a good chance to test this matter of possession; the suggestion nimbly and sweetly recommends itself to my fancy. But since I was your pioneer to-night, I'll even rest until Zoïlus has finished; then, let us all start fairly.

Zoïlus (*a few minutes later*). If this is at all good, it is not because of labor. I had an easier task than the Gannet. (*Reads.*)

THE PROMISSORY NOTE.

In the lonesome latter years,
    (Fatal years!)
To the dropping of my tears
Danced the mad and mystic spheres
In a rounded, reeling rune,
    'Neath the moon,
To the dripping and the dropping of my tears.

Ah, my soul is swathed in gloom,
    (Ulalume!)
In a dim Titanic tomb,
For my gaunt and gloomy soul

Ponders o'er the penal scroll,
O'er the parchment (not a rhyme),
Out of place, — out of time, —
I am shredded, shorn, unshifty,
    (O, the fifty!)
And the days have passed, the three,
    Over me!
And the debit and the credit are as one to him and me!

'T was the random runes I wrote
At the bottom of the note,
    (Wrote and freely
    Gave to Greeley,)
In the middle of the night,
In the mellow, moonless night,
When the stars were out of sight,
When my pulses, like a knell,
    (Israfel!)
Danced with dim and dying fays
O'er the ruins of my days,
O'er the dimeless, timeless days,
When the fifty, drawn at thirty,
Seeming thrifty, yet the dirty
Lucre of the market, was the most that I could raise!

Fiends controlled it,
    (Let him hold it!)
Devils held for me the inkstand and the pen;
Now the days of grace are o'er,
    (Ah, Lenore!)
I am but as other men:
What is time, time, time,
To my rare and runic rhyme,

>   To my random, reeling rhyme,
>   By the sands along the shore,
> Where the tempest whispers, "Pay him!" and I answer, "Nevermore!"

GALAHAD. What do you mean by the reference to Greeley?

ZOÏLUS. I thought everybody had heard that Greeley's only autograph of Poe was a signature to a promissory note for fifty dollars. He offers to sell it for half the money. Now, I don't mean to be wicked, and to do nothing with the dead except bone 'em, but when such a cue pops into one's mind, what is one to do?

THE ANCIENT. O, I think you're still within decent limits! There was a congenital twist about poor Poe. We can't entirely condone his faults, yet we stretch our charity so as to cover as much as possible. His poetry has a hectic flush, a strange, fascinating, narcotic quality, which belongs to him alone. Baudelaire and Swinburne after him have been trying to surpass him by increasing the dose; but his Muse is the natural Pythia, inheriting her convulsions, while they eat all sorts of insane roots to produce theirs.

GALAHAD (*eagerly*). Did you ever know him?

THE ANCIENT. I met him two or three times, heard him lecture once (his enunciation was exquisite), and saw him now and then in Broadway,— enough to satisfy me that there were two men in him: one, a refined gentleman, an aspiring soul, an artist among those who had little sense of literary art; the other —

ZOÏLUS. Go on!

THE ANCIENT. "Built his nest with the birds of

Night." No more of that! Now let us all invoke the demigod, Browning.

GALAHAD. It will be a task.

ZOÏLUS. I don't think so; it's even simpler than what we've done. Why, Browning's manner is as distinctly his own as Carlyle's, and sometimes as wilfully artificial. In fact, he is so peculiarly himself that no younger poet has dared to imitate his fashion of speech, although many a one tries to follow him in the choice and treatment of subjects. Browning is the most dramatic of poets since Shakespeare; don't you think so, Ancient?

THE ANCIENT. In manner and language, perhaps. I should prefer to call him a psychologist. His subtile studies of all varieties of character are wonderful, if you look at the substance only; but every one of them, from first to last, speaks with the voice of Browning. Take "The Ring and the Book," for instance, — and I consider it one of the most original and excellent poems in the English language, — and in each of the twelve divisions you will find exactly the same interruptions, parentheses, ellipses, the same coinage of illustration and play of recondite hints under what is expressed. I should guess that he writes very rapidly, and concerns himself little with any objective theories of art. You ought to copy his manner easily enough.

ZOÏLUS. I can. I have caught the idea already. (*He takes a pencil and writes rapidly.* GALAHAD *and the* GANNET *also begin to write, but slowly.*)

THE CHORUS (*to* THE ANCIENT). Why don't you begin?

THE ANCIENT. I was deliberating; what a range of

forms there is!" He is as inexhaustible as Raphael, and he always expresses the same sense of satisfaction in his work. Well, anything will do for a subject. (*Writes.*)

ZOÏLUS (*after a few minutes*). Hearken! I must read at once, or I shall go on writing forever; it bewilders me. (*Reads.*)

> Who *wills*, may hear Sordello's story told
> By Robert Browning: warm? (you ask) or cold?
> But just so much as seemeth to enhance —
> The start being granted, onward goes the dance
> To its own music — the poem's inward sense;
> So, by its verity .... nay, no pretence
> Avails your self-created bards, and thus
> By just the chance of half a hair to us,
> If understood .... but what the odds to you,
> Who, with no obligations to pursue
> Scant tracks of thought, if such, indeed, there be
> In this one poem, — stay, my friend, and see
> Whether you note that creamy tint of flesh,
> Softer than bivalve pink, impearled and fresh,
> Just where the small o' the back goes curving down
> To orbic muscles .... ha! that sidelong frown
> Pursing the eye, and folded, deeply cleft
> I' the nostril's edge, as though contempt were left
> Just o'er the line that bounds indifference.....
> But here's the test of any closer sense
> (You follow me?) such as I started with;
> And there be minds that seek the very pith,
> Crowd close, bore deep, push far, and reach the light
> Through league-long tunnels —

GALAHAD (*interrupting*). But that *is* Sordello you're reading!

ZoÏlus. Yes, mine. I am one of the few who have bored their way through that amazing work. Browning's "Sordello" (if you ever read it, you will remember) begins with something about "Pentapolin o' the Naked Arm." It is not any particular passage, but the manner of the whole poem which I've tried to reproduce; a little exaggerated, to be sure, but not much. Now, I call this perplexity, not profundity. Wasn't it the Swedish poet, Tegner, who said, "The obscurely uttered is the obscurely thought"?

The Ancient. Yes; and it is true in regard to poetry, however the case may be with metaphysics. But we have a right to be vexed with Browning, when, in the dedicatory letter to the new edition of "Sordello," he says that he had taken pains to make the work something "which the many *might*, instead of what the few *must*, like," but, after all, did not choose to publish the revised copy. There is a touch of arrogance in this expression which I should rather not have encountered. The "*must*" which he flings at the few is far more offensive than utter indifference to all readers would have been; and not even those few can make us accept "Sordello." However, *multum creavit* is as good a plea as *multum dilexit*. Browning has a royal brain, and we owe him too much to bear malice against him. Only, we must not encourage our masters in absolute rule, or they will become tyrants.

ZoÏlus. I don't acknowledge any masters!

The Ancient. We all know that. Now, Galahad, what have you done?

Galahad (*reads*):—

BY THE SEA.

(Mutatis mutandis.)

I.

Is it life or is it death?
   A whiff of the cool salt scum,
As the whole sea puffed its breath
   Against you, — blind and dumb,
This way it answereth.

II.

Nearer the sands it shows
   Spotted and leprous tints:
But stay! yon fisher knows
   Rock-tokens, which evince
How high the tide arose.

III.

How high? In you and me
   'T was falling then, I think;
Open your heart's eyes, see
   From just so slight a chink
The chasm that now must be.

IV.

You sighed and shivered then,
   Blue ecstasies of June
Around you, shouts of fishermen,
   Sharp wings of sea-gulls, soon
To dip — the clock struck ten!

V.

Was it the cup too full,
   To carry it you grew
Too faint, the wine's hue dull,
   (Dulness, misjudged untrue!)
Love's flower unfit to cull?

VI.

You should have held me fast
   One moment, stopped my pace,
Crushed down the feeble, vast
   Suggestions of embrace,
And so be crowned at last.

VII.

But now! .... Bare-legged and brown
   Bait-diggers delve the sand,
Tramp i' the sunshine down
   Burnt-ochre vestured land,
And yonder stares the town.

VIII.

A heron screams! I shut
   This book of scurf and scum,
Its final page uncut;
   The sea-beast, blind and dumb,
Done with his bellowing? All but!

THE GANNET. It seems we have all hit upon the obvious characteristics, especially those which are most confusing. There is something very like that in the "*Dramatis Personæ*," or there seems to be. Now, I wonder how my attempt will strike you? (*Reads.*)

ANGELO ORDERS HIS DINNER.

I, Angelo, obese, black-garmented,
Respectable, much in demand, well fed
With mine own larder's dainties, — where, indeed,
Such cakes of myrrh or fine alyssum seed,
Thin as a mallow-leaf, embrowned o' the top,
Which, cracking, lets the ropy, trickling drop
Of sweetness touch your tongue, or potted nests
Which my recondite recipe invests
With cold conglomerate tidbits — ah, the bill!
(You say,) but given it were mine to fill
My chests, the case so put were yours, we'll say,
(This counter, here, your post, as mine to-day,)
And you 've an eye to luxuries, what harm
In smoothing down your palate with the charm
Yourself concocted? There we issue take;
And see! as thus across the rim I break
This puffy paunch of glazed embroidered cake,
So breaks, through use, the lust of watering chaps
And craveth plainness: do I so? Perhaps;
But that 's my secret. Find me such a man
As Lippo yonder, built upon the plan
Of heavy storage, double-navelled, fat
From his own giblets' oils, an Ararat
Uplift o'er water, sucking rosy draughts
From Noah's vineyard, — . . . crisp, enticing wafts
You kitchen now emits, which to your sense
Somewhat abate the fear of old events,
Qualms to the stomach, — I, you see, am slow
Unnecessary duties to forego, —
You understand? A venison haunch, *haut gout*,

Ducks that in Cimbrian olives mildly stew,
And sprigs of anise, might one's teeth provoke
To taste, and so we wear the complex yoke
Just as it suits, — my liking, I confess,
More to receive, and to partake no less,
Still more obese, while through thick adipose
Sensation shoots, from testing tongue to toes
Far off, dim-conscious, at the body's verge,
Where the froth-whispers of its waves emerge
On the untasting sand. Stay, now! a seat
Is bare: I, Angelo, will sit and eat.

THE CHORUS. There's no mistaking any of them!

THE ANCIENT. And yet what a wealth of forms and moods there is left! You have only touched the poet on two or three of his shifting sides. Whoever should hear these imitations first, and then take up the original works, would recognize certain fashions here and there, but he would be wholly unprepared for the special best qualities of Browning.

THE CHORUS. How, then, have *you* fared?

THE ANCIENT. I'm afraid I've violated the very law I laid down at the beginning. But I took the first notion that came into my head, and I could not possibly make it either all imitation or all burlesque. However, hear, and then punish me as you like! (*Reads.*)

ON THE TRACK.

Where the crags are close, and the railway-curve
    Begins to swerve
From its straight-shot course i' the level plain
    To the hills again,

At the end of the twilight, when you mark
      The denser dark

Blown by the wind from the heights, that make
      A cold, coiled snake
Round the shuddering world, as a Midgards-orm-
      like, sinuous form,—
With scant-cut hosen, jacket in hands,
      The small boy stands.

Clipt by the iron ways, shiny and straight,
      You see him wait,
'Twixt the coming thunder and the rock,
      To fend the shock,
As a mite should stay, with its wriggling force,
      A planet's course.

Even as he dances, leaps, and stoops,
      The black train swoops
Up from the level: wave jacket, cry!
      Must all then die?
Sweating, the small boy smiles again;
      He has stopped the train!

GALAHAD. Well, that somehow suggests to me two poems: his "Love among the Ruins," and the "Incident of the French Camp," yet it is not an imitation of either. I should only apply to it the same criticism as to my own,—that it gives no hint of Browning's subtile and ingenious way of dealing with the simplest subjects. He seems always to seek some other than the ordinary and natural point of view. I believe he could change "Mother Hubbard" and "Kits, cats, sacks, and wives" into profound psychological poems.

THE ANCIENT. Now, why did n't you say that before we began? I might have made, at least, a more grotesque failure. But, O Gambrinus! our glasses have been empty this hour. Ring for the waiter, Galahad; let us refresh our wearied virtue, and depart!

OMNES (*touching glasses*). To be continued!

[*Exeunt.*

NIGHT THE SECOND.

THE friends came together again in the Lions' Den, a little earlier than their wont; but they did not immediately take up the chief diversion of the evening. In intellectual, as in physical acrobatics, the joints must be gradually made flexible, and the muscles warm and elastic, by lighter feats; so the conversation began as mere skylarking and mutual chaffing, as empty and evanescent, when you attempt to catch it, as the foam-ripples on a swift stream. But Galahad had something on his mind; he had again read portions of the "Earthly Paradise," and insisted that the atmosphere of the poems was not gray and overcast, but charged with a golden, luminous mist, like that of the Indian summer. Finally, he asked the Ancient, —

"Granting the force of your impression, might not much of it come from some want of harmony between your mood or temper of mind and the author's? In that case, it would not be abstractly just."

THE ANCIENT. I don't think that we often can be "abstractly just" towards contemporary poets; we either exalt or abase them too much. For we and they breathe either the same or opposite currents in the intellectual atmosphere of the time, and there can be no impartial estimate until those winds have blown over. This is precisely the reason why you sometimes think me indifferent, when I am only trying to shove myself as far off as the next generation; at least, to get a little outside of the fashions and whims and prejudices of this day. American authors, and also their publishers, are often charged with an over-concern for the opinion of the English literary journals. I think their interest quite natural —

ZOÏLUS (*with energy*). Now, you surely are not going to justify that sycophantic respect for the judgment of men who know so much less than we do of our own literature!

THE ANCIENT. I condemn *all* sycophancy, even to the great, triumphant, overwhelming American spirit! But, until we have literary criticism of a more purely objective character in this country, — until our critics learn to separate their personal tastes and theories from their estimate of the executive and artistic quality of the author; or, which amounts to the same thing, to set this quality, this creative principle, higher than the range of themes and opinions, — the author will look to the judgment of critics, whose distance and whose very want of acquaintance with our prejudices and passions assure him of a certain amount of impartiality. The feeling is reciprocal; I venture to say that an intelligent American criticism has more weight with an English author than that of one of his own Reviews.

ZOÏLUS. Do you mean to say that we have *no* genuine criticism?

The Ancient. By no means; we have some that is admirable. But it is only recognized at its true value by a very small class; the great reading public is blissfully ignorant of its existence. It adds to the confusion, that many of our writers have no definite ideas of literary excellence apart from the effect which immediately follows their work; and readers are thus actually misled by those who should guide them. Why, a year ago, the most popular book in the whole country was one which does not even belong to literature; and the most popular poem of late years was written, not from a poetic, but from a high moral, inspiration! Somebody must set up a true æsthetic standard; it is high time this were done, and a better criticism must be the first step.

The Gannet. Why don't you undertake it yourself?

The Ancient. I'm too fond of comfort. Think what a hornet's-nest I should thrust my hand into? Moreover, I doubt whether one could force such interests beyond their natural growth; we are still suffering from the intellectual demoralization which the war left behind it. But, where's the hat? We are spoiling ourselves by all this serious prose. Let us throw in a few more names, and try our luck again.

(*They draw the lots as before.*)

The Gannet. John Keats! How shall I wear his mantle?

Zoïlus. I'm crushed, buried under an avalanche of, — well, not much, after all. Don't ask me who it is, until I try my hand. You would confuse me with your laughter.

The Ancient. I shall keep mine specially for you, Zoïlus.

Galahad. I have drawn one of the names I wrote myself; but you have already so demoralized me, that I will try to parody him as heartily as if I did n't like his poetry.

The Ancient. You are getting on. But I think the Gannet ought to draw another name; it is best not to go back of our own day and generation. I propose that we limit ourselves to the poets who stand nearer to our own minds, under whom, or beside whom, or above whom (as each chooses to estimate himself), we have grown and are now growing. The further we withdraw from this atmosphere, the more artificial must our imitations be.

The Gannet. Let it pass this once, I pray thee, for I have caught my idea! But, even taking your limitation, who is nearer us than Keats? Not alone in his own person, though there he stands among us; he is in Tennyson, in Morris, in Swinburne, and, more remotely, in the earlier poems of Browning and Lowell, besides a host of small rhymers. He still approaches us, while Shelley and Byron withdraw. I think it's a fair exception; and if you won't admit it, I 'll take the sense of the company.

Omnes. Go on!

(*All write busily for fifteen minutes, except* The Ancient *who talks in a lower tone to* The Chorus.)

The Gannet (*looking up*). Zoïlus, you were ready first.

Zoïlus. Could you guess whom I represent?

The Gannet. Tupper?

ZOÏLUS. He? he is his own best parody. No; it is a lyrical inanity, which once was tolerably famous. The Ancient's rule as to what is properly parodiable does n't apply here; for it is neither excellent nor imbecile. I think I had the right to reject the name, but I have tried to see whether a respectable jingle of words, expressing ordinary and highly proper feelings, can be so imitated as to be recognized. Here it is. (*Reads.*)

OBITUARY.

ON THE DEATH OF THE REV. ELIJAH W. BATEY.

Ay, bear him to his sainted rest,
   Ye mourners, but be calm!
Instead of dirge and sable crest,
   Raise ye thanksgiving psalm!
For he was old and full of years,
   The grandsire of your souls:
Then check ye now your heaving tears,
   And quench the sigh that rolls!

Ye heard him from yon pulpit preach,
   For sixty years and more,
Still battering with unwearied speech
   The ceiling, pews, and floor;
As, hour by hour, his periods fell,
   Your pious hopes arose,
And each one murmured, "All is well,"
   Long ere the sermon's close.

Think ye the voice that spake so long
   Can anywhere be dumb?

Before him went a goodly throng,
  And wait for him to come.
He preaches still, in other spheres,
  To saved and patient souls ;
Then, mourners, check your heaving tears,
  And quench the sigh that rolls !

OMNES (*shouting*). Mrs. Sigourney !

ZOÏLUS. I *have* succeeded, then ! But, O my friends, is the success a thing over which I should rejoice ? Do not, I beg of you, do not congratulate me !

GALAHAD. Come, now, don't abuse good old Mother Sigourney ! For a long time she was almost our only woman-poet ; and I insist that she was not a mere echo of Felicia Hemans.

ZOÏLUS (*ironically*). Of course not ! None but herself could ever have written that exquisite original poem, "On Finding a Shred of Linen." One passage I can never forget : —

  "Methinks I scan
Some idiosyncrasy, which marks thee out
A defunct pillow-case."

GALAHAD. You are incorrigible ; but we wait for the Gannet and the idea he has caught.

THE GANNET. It was better in anticipation than it seems after execution. However, Keats is too dainty a spirit to be possessed in a few minutes. (*Reads.*)

ODE ON A JAR OF PICKLES.

I.

A sweet, acidulous, down-reaching thrill
   Pervades my sense: I seem to see or hear
The lushy garden-grounds of Greenwich Hill
   In autumn, when the crispy leaves are sere:
And odors haunt me of remotest spice
   From the Levant or musky-aired Cathay,
Or from the saffron-fields of Jericho,
     Where everything is nice:
   The more I sniff, the more I swoon away,
And what else mortal palate craves, forego.

II.

Odors unsmelled are keen, but those I smell
   Are keener; wherefore let me sniff again!
Enticing walnuts, I have known ye well
   In youth, when pickles were a passing pain;
Unwitting youth, that craves the candy stem,
   And sugar-plums to olives doth prefer,
And even licks the pots of marmalade
     When sweetness clings to them:
   But now I dream of ambergris and myrrh,
Tasting these walnuts in the poplar shade.

III.

Lo! hoarded coolness in the heart of noon,
   Plucked with its dew, the cucumber is here,
As to the Dryad's parching lips a boon,
   And crescent bean-pods, unto Bacchus dear;
And, last of all, the pepper's pungent globe,
   The scarlet dwelling of the sylph of fire,

Provoking purple draughts; and, surfeited,
    I cast my trailing robe
O'er my pale feet, touch up my tuneless lyre,
And twist the Delphic wreath to suit my head.

IV.

Here shall my tongue in other wise be soured
    Than fretful men's in parched and palsied days;
And, by the mid-May's dusky leaves embowered
    Forget the fruitful blame, the scanty praise.
No sweets to them who sweet themselves were born,
    Whose natures ooze with lucent saccharine;
Who, with sad repetition soothly cloyed,
      The lemon-tinted morn
    Enjoy, and for acetic darkness pine:
Wake I, or sleep? The pickle-jar is void.

ZOÏLUS. Not to be mistaken; but you have almost stepped over the bounds of our plan. Those two odes of Keats are too immediately suggested, though I find that only two lines are actually parodied. I agree with the Ancient; let us stick to the authors of our own day! Galahad, you look mysterious; are we to guess your singer from the echo?

GALAHAD. Are you all ready to hear me chant, in rare and rhythmic redundancy, the viciousness of virtue?

THE CHORUS. O, Swinburne! chant away!

GALAHAD (*reads*):—

THE LAY OF MACARONI.

As a wave that steals when the winds are stormy
    From creek to cove of the curving shore,

Buffeted, blown, and broken before me,
  Scattered and spread to its sunlit core;
As a dove that dips in the dark of maples
  To sip the sweetness of shelter and shade,
I kneel in thy nimbus, O noon of Naples,
  I bathe in thine beauty, by thee embayed!

What is it ails me that I should sing of her?
  The queen of the flashes and flames that were!
Yea, I have felt the shuddering sting of her,
  The flower-sweet throat and the hands of her!
I have swayed and sung to the sound of her psalters,
  I have danced her dances of dizzy delight,
I have hallowed mine hair to the horns of her altars,
  Between the nightingale's song and the night!

What is it, Queen, that now I should do for thee?
  What is it now I should ask at thine hands?
Blow of the trumpets thine children once blew for thee?
  Break from thine feet and thine bosom the bands?
Nay, as sweet as the songs of Leone Leoni,
  And gay as her garments of gem-sprinkled gold,
She gives me mellifluous, mild macaroni,
  The choice of her children when cheeses are old!

And over me hover, as if by the wings of it,
  Frayed in the furnace by flame that is fleet,
The curious coils and the strenuous strings of it,
  Dropping, diminishing down, as I eat:
Lo! and the beautiful Queen, as she brings of it,
  Lifts me the links of the limitless chain,
Bidding mine mouth chant the splendidest things of it,
  Out of the wealth of my wonderful brain!

Behold! I have done it: my stomach is smitten
  With sweets of the surfeit her hands have unrolled.
Italia, mine cheeks with thine kisses are bitten:
  I am broken with beauty, stabbed, slaughtered, and sold!
No man of thine millions is more macaronied,
  Save mighty Mazzini, than musical Me:
The souls of the Ages shall stand as astonied,
  And faint in the flame I am fanning for thee!

THE ANCIENT (*laughing*). O Galahad, I can fancy your later remorse. It is not a year since you were absolutely Swinburne-mad, and I hardly dared, in your presence, to object even to "Anactoria" and "Dolores." I *would not* encourage you, then, for I saw you were carried away by the wild rush of the rhythm, and the sparkle of epithets which were partly new and seemed wholly splendid; but now I will confess to you that as a purely rhythmical genius I look on Swinburne as a phenomenon in literature.

GALAHAD (*eagerly*). Then you admit that he is great?

THE ANCIENT. Not as you mean. I have been waiting for his ferment to settle, as in the case of Keats and Shelley; but there are no signs of it in his last volume. How splendidly the mind of Keats precipitated its crudity and redundancy, and clarified into the pure wine of "Hyperion"! In Shelley's case the process was slower, but it was steadily going on; you will find the same thing in Schiller, in Dryden, and many other poets, therefore I mean to reserve my judgment in Swinburne's case, and wait, at least until his next work is published. Meanwhile, I grant that he has enriched our English lyric poetry with some new and admirable forms.

The Gannet. He has certainly made a "sensation" in the literary world; does that indicate nothing?

The Ancient. That depends. I declare it seems to me as if the general taste were not quite healthy. To a very large class reading has become a form of lazy luxury, and such readers are not satisfied without a new great poet, every four or five years. Then, too, there has been an amazing deal of trash written about the *coming* authors, — what they should be, how they must write, and the like; and so those luxurious readers are all the time believing they have discovered one of the tribe. Why, let a man take a thought as old as Confucius, and put it into some strange, jerky, convulsed form, and you will immediately hear the cry, "How wonderful! how original!" You all remember the case of Alexander Smith; it seems incredible, now, that the simulated passion and forced sentiment of his "Life-Drama" should have been accepted as real, yet, because of this book, he was hailed as a second Shakespeare. This hunger of the luxurious reader for new flavors is a dangerous thing for young poets.

Zoïlus. I almost think I hear my own voice. We don't often agree so thoroughly.

The Ancient. So much the better. I wonder if you'll be as well satisfied with the task I have in store for you; here is the name. (*Giving him the slip of paper.*)

Zoïlus. Emerson! I think I can guess why.

The Ancient. Yes, I remember what you wrote when "Brahma" was first published, and what you said to Galahad the other evening. I confess I was amazed, at the time, that the newspapers should so innocently betray their ignorance. There was a universal cry of "incomprehensible!" when the meaning of the poem was perfectly plain. In fact, there are few authors so transparently clear, barring a few idiosyncrasies of expression, which one soon learns, as just Emerson.

ZOÏLUS. Then explain to me those lines from "Alphonso of Castile":—

> "Hear you then, celestial fellows!
> Fits not to be over-zealous;
> Stends not to work on the clean jump,
> And wine and brains perpetual pump!"

THE ANCIENT. That is simply baldness of language (which Emerson sometimes mistakes for humor), not obscurity. I will not explain it! Read the whole poem over again, and I'm sure you will not need to ask me. But now, to your work! Who will draw again?

THE GANNET (*drawing*). Ha! A friend, this time; and I wish he were here with us. Nobody would take more kindly to our fun than he.

GALAHAD. I shall try no more, to-night. My imitation of Swinburne has exhausted me. I felt, while writing, as Zoïlus did when he was imitating Browning,— as if I could have gone on and on forever! Really there is some sort of possession or demoniac influence in these experiments. They fascinate me, and yet I feel as if a spirit foreign to my own had seized me.

THE ANCIENT. Take another cigar! I wish we had the Meleager, or the Farnese torso, here; five minutes of either would surround you with a different atmosphere. I know precisely how it affects you. Thirty years ago, O Tempus Edax, must I say *thirty?* when I dreamed hot dreams of fame, and walked the streets in a mild delirium, pondering over the great and godlike powers pent within me, I had the same chills and fevers. I'm not laughing at you, my dear Galahad; God forbid! I only pray that there may be more vitality in the seeds which your dreams cover, than in mine. Waiter! Our glasses are empty.

(Zoïlus *and the* Gannet *continue to write: meantime, fresh glasses of beer are brought, and there is a brief silence.*)

Zoïlus. I suspect the Ancient will want to knock me on the head for this. (*Reads.*)

ALL OR NOTHING.

Whoso answers my questions
    Knoweth more than me;
Hunger is but knowledge
    In a less degree:
Prophet, priest, and poet
    Oft prevaricate,
And the surest sentence
    Hath the greatest weight.

When upon my gaiters
    Drops the morning dew,
Somewhat of Life's riddle
    Soaks my spirit through.
I am buskined by the goddess
    Of Monadnock's crest,
And my wings extended
    Touch the East and West.

Or ever coal was hardened
  In the cells of earth,
Or flowed the founts of Bourbon,
  Lo! I had my birth.
I am crowned coeval
  With the Saurian eggs,
And my fancy firmly
  Stands on its own legs.

Wouldst thou know the secret
  Of the barberry-bush,
Catch the slippery whistle
  Of the moulting thrush,
Dance upon the mushrooms,
  Dive beneath the sea,
Or anything else remarkable,
  Thou must follow me!

THE ANCIENT. Well, you have read somewhat more than I imagined, Zoïlus. This is a fair imitation of the manner of some of Emerson's earlier poems; but you may take heart, Galahad, if you fear the power of association, for not one of the inimitable, imperishable passages has been suggested.

ZOÏLUS. Now, seriously, do you mean to say that there are such?

THE ANCIENT.

"Still on the seeds of all he made
  The rose of beauty burns;
Through times that wear, and forms that fade,
  Immortal youth returns."

GALAHAD (*drawing a long breath*). How beautiful!
THE ANCIENT.

"Thou canst not wave thy staff in air,
 Or dip thy paddle in the lake,
But it carves the bow of Beauty there,
 And the ripples in rhyme the oar forsake."

ZOÏLUS. *Peccavi!*

THE ANCIENT. Then I will lock up my half-unbolted thunders. The Master does not need my vindication; and I should do him a poor service by trying to drive any one towards the recognition of his deserts, when all who think for themselves must come, sooner or later, to know him.

THE GANNET. But I never saw those stanzas!

THE ANCIENT. Yet they are printed for all the world. The secret is simply this: Emerson cut from his limbs, long ago, the old theological fetters, as every independent thinker *must*. Those who run along in the ruts made by their grandfathers, unable to appreciate the exquisite fibre of his intellect, the broad and grand eclecticism of his taste, suspect a heresy in every sentence which they are too coarsely textured to understand. No man of our day habitually lives in a purer region of thought.

ZOÏLUS (*looking at his watch*). Now, we must know what the Gannet has been doing.

THE GANNET. My name was Edmund Clarence Stedman.

THE ANCIENT. One of the younger tribes, with some of whom I'm not so familiar. I have caught many of his "fugitives," in their flight, finding them of a kind sure to stay where they touch, instead of being blown quietly on until they pass forever out of the world. There's a fine masculine vibration in his lines: he sings in the major key, which young poets generally do not. I'd be willing to bet that your imitation has a sportive, not a solemn, character.

THE GANNET. Why, in spite of your disclaimer, you're not so ignorant. Your guess is right: therefore, listen! (*Reads.*)

THE GOLD-ROOM.

AN IDYL.

They come from mansions far up-town,
    And from their country villas,
And some, Charybdis' gulf whirls down,
    And some fall into Scylla's.
Lo! here young Paris climbs the stairs
    As if their slope were Ida's,
And here his golden touch declares
    The ass's ears of Midas.

It seems a Bacchic, brawling rout
    To every business-scorner,
But such, methinks, must be an "out,"
    Or has not made a "corner."
In me the rhythmic gush revives;
    I feel a classic passion:
We, also, lead Arcadian lives,
    Though in a Broad-Street fashion.

Old Battos, here, 's a leading bull,
    And Diomed a bear is,

>   And near them, shearing bankers' wool,
>   Strides the Tiltonian Charis;
>   And Atys, there, has gone to smash,
>   His every bill protested,
>   While Cleon's eyes with comfort flash, —
>   *I* have his funds invested!
>
>   Mehercle! 't is the same thing yet
>   As in the days of Pindar:
>   The Isthmian race, the dust and sweat,
>   The prize — why, what 's to hinder?
>   And if I twang my lyre at times,
>   They did so then, I reckon;
>   That man 's the best at modern rhymes
>   Whom you can draw a check on!

OMNES (*clapping their hands*). Bravo!

THE ANCIENT. To think of Stedman's being the only voice in our literature which comes out of the business crowds of the whole country! The man who can spend his days in a purely material atmosphere, and sing at night, has genuine pluck in him. It 's enough to make any green poet, who wails about the cruel world, and the harsh realities of life, and the beautiful realm of the ideal, ashamed of himself!

GALAHAD (*annoyed*). You don't mean as much as you say! Every poet, green or not, must have faith in an ideal.

THE ANCIENT (*gently*). Ay, but if it make him

>   " Pamper the coward heart
>   With feelings all too delicate for use,"

as Coleridge translates Schiller, it is a deceit and a snare to him. Your Shakespeare, Dante, Cervantes, Goethe, were made of different clay.

Zoïlus. Here's to their sublime Shades, wherever they may be wandering! Out, to the last drop! We are in the small hours; the *Donnerwetters!* are all silent in the saloon, and Karl Schäfer is probably snoring over his counter, waiting for us. Come! [*Exeunt.*

NIGHT THE THIRD.

WHEN the sportive tilting with light lances, the reciprocal, good-natured chaffing, in which the members of the Club were wont to indulge on coming together, had subsided, the conversation took the following turn:

ZOÏLUS (*to* THE ANCIENT). I've been considering what you said the last time, about the prevalent literary taste not being entirely healthy. How far would you apply that verdict to the authors? Their relative popularity is your only gauge for the character of the readers.

THE ANCIENT. I don't think I had any individual authors in my mind, at the time. But a great deal of all modern literature is ephemeral, created from day to day to supply a certain definite demand, and sinking out of sight, sooner or later. Nine readers out of ten make no distinction between this ephemeral material and the few works which really belong to our literary history; that is, they confound the transitory with the permanent authors.

ZOÏLUS. So far, I agree with you. Now the inference would be that those nine readers, who lack the finer judgment, and who, of course, represent the prevalent taste, are responsible for the success of the transitory authors. But they do not make the latter; they do not even dictate the character of their works: hence the school, no matter how temporary it may be, must be founded by the authors, — which obliges us to admit a certain degree of originality and power.

THE ANCIENT. I see where you are going; let us have no reasoning in a ring, I pray you! If you admit the two classes of authors, it is enough. I have already seen one generation forgotten, and I fancy I now see the second slipping the cables of their craft, and making ready to drop down stream with the ebb-tide. I remember, for instance, that in 1840 there were many well-known and tolerably popular names, which are never heard now. Byron and Mrs. Hemans then gave the tone to poetry, and Scott, Bulwer, and Cooper to fiction. Willis was, by all odds, the most popular American author; Longfellow was not known by the multitude, Emerson was only "that Transcendentalist," and Whittier "that Abolitionist." We young men used to talk of Rufus Dawes, and Charles Fenno Hoffman, and Grenville Mellen, and Brainard, and Sands. Why, we even had a hope that something wonderful would come out of Chivers!

OMNES. Chivers?

THE ANCIENT. Have you never heard of Chivers? He is a phenomenon!

THE GANNET. Doesn't Poe speak of him somewhere?

THE ANCIENT. To be sure. Poe finished the ruin of him which Shelley began. Dr. Thomas Holley Chivers, of Georgia, author of "Virginalia," "The Lost Pleiad," "Facets of Diamond," and "Eonchs of Ruby!"

Zoïlus. What! Come, now, this is only a *ben trovato*.

The Ancient. Also of "Nacoochee, the Beautiful Star"; and there was still another volume, — six in all! The British Museum has the only complete set of his works. I speak the sober truth, Zoïlus; a friend of mine has three of the volumes, and I can show them to you. One of the finest images in modern poetry is in his "Apollo": —

"Like cataracts of adamant, uplifted into mountains,
  Making oceans metropolitan, for the splendor of the dawn!"

Zoïlus. Incredible!

The Ancient. I remember also a stanza of his "Rosalie Lee": —

"Many mellow Cydonian suckets,
  Sweet apples, anthosmial, divine,
From the ruby-rimmed beryline buckets,
  Star-gemmed, lily-shaped, hyaline;
Like the sweet golden goblet found growing
  On the wild emerald cucumber-tree,
Rich, brilliant, like chrysoprase glowing,
  Was my beautiful Rosalie Lee!"

Zoïlus. Hold, hold! I can endure no more.

The Ancient. You see what comes of a fashion in literature. There was many a youth in those days who made attempts just as idiotic, in the columns of country papers; and perhaps the most singular circumstance was, that very few readers laughed at them. Why, there are expressions, epithets, images, which run all over the land, and sometimes last for a generation. I once discovered that with both the English and German poets of a hundred years ago, evening is always called *brown*, and morning either *rosy* or *purple*. Just now the fashion runs to jewelry; we have ruby lips, and topaz light, and sapphire seas, and diamond air. Mrs. Browning even says: —

" Her *cheek's pale opal* burnt with a red and restless spark!"

What sort of a cheek must that be? Then we have such a wealth of gorgeous color as never was seen before, — no quiet half-tints, but pure pigments, laid on with a pallet-knife. Really, I sometimes feel a distinct sense of fatigue at the base of the optic nerve, after reading a magazine story. The besetting sin of the popular — not the best — authors is the intense.

ZoÏlus. Why do you call intensity of expression a sin?

The Ancient. I mean intensity of *epithet:* the strongest expression is generally the briefest and barest. Take the old ballads of any people, and you will find few adjectives. The singer says: "He laughed; she wept." Perhaps the poet of a more civilized age might say: "He laughed in scorn; she turned away and shed tears of disappointment." But nowadays, the ambitious young writer must produce something like this: "A hard, fiendish laugh, scornful and pitiless, forced its passage from his throat through the lips that curled in mockery of her appeal; she covered her despairing face, and a gust and whirlwind of sorrowing agony burst forth in her irresistible tears!"

OMNES (*clapping their hands*). Go on! Go on!

THE ANCIENT. It is enough of the Bowery, for to-night.

GALAHAD. O, you forget the intenser life of our day! I see the exaggeration of which you speak, but I believe something of it comes from the struggle to express more. All our senses have grown keener, our natures respond more delicately, and to a greater range of influences, than those of the generations before us. There is a finer moral development; our aims in life have become spiritualized; we may have less power, less energy of genius, but we move towards higher and purer goals.

ZOÏLUS. The writers of Queen Anne's time might have compared themselves in the same way with their predecessors in Charles II.'s. What if your own poems should be considered coarse and immoral a hundred years hence?

GALAHAD (*bewildered*). What has that to do with the question?

THE ANCIENT. Only this; that there are eternal laws of Art, to which the moral and spiritual aspirations of the author, which are generally relative to his own or the preceding age, must conform, if they would also become eternal.

THE GANNET. Very fine, indeed; but you are all forgetting our business.

ZOÏLUS. Let us first add a fresh supply of names.

THE GANNET. Write them yourself; we shall otherwise repeat.

(Zoïlus *writes a dozen or more slips, whereupon they draw.*)

Galahad. Dante Rossetti!

Zoïlus. I have Barry Cornwall.

The Gannet. And I — Whittier.

Omnes. Whittier must not be parodied.

Galahad (*earnestly*). Draw another name!

The Ancient. Why?

Galahad. There is at once an evidence of what I said! Where are your jewelry and colors? On the other side, where will you find an intenser faith, a more ardent aspiration for truth and good? The moral and spiritual element is so predominant in him, — so wedded for time and eternity to his genius as a poet, — that you cannot imitate him without seeming to slight, or in some way offend, what should be as holy to us as to him!

The Ancient (*laying his hand on* Galahad's *shoulder*). My dear boy, Whittier deserves all the love and reverence you are capable of giving him. He is just as fine an illustration of my side of the question: his poetic art has refined and harmonized that moral quality in his nature, which, many years ago, made his poetry seem partisan, and, therefore, not unmixed poetry. But the alloy (in a poetic sense, only) has been melted out in the pure and steady flame of his intellect, and the preacher in him has now his rightful authority because he no longer governs the poet. As for those poems which exhale devotion and aspiration as naturally as a violet exhales odor, there is no danger of the Gannet imitating them; he has not the power even if he had the will. But Whittier has also written —

The Gannet. Don't you see I'm hard at work?

What do you mean by dictating what I may or may not do? I am already well launched, and (*declaiming*) "I seek no change; and, least of all, such change as you would give me!"

THE ANCIENT. I can't help you, Galahad; go on with your own work now. I have drawn one of the youngsters, this time, and mean to turn him over to you when you have slaughtered Rossetti.

GALAHAD. Who is he?

THE ANCIENT. A brother near your throne.

ZOÏLUS (*to* THE ANCIENT). I have done Barry Cornwall; it's an easy task. He is nearly always very brief. His are not even short swallow-flights of song, but little hops from one twig to another. While Galahad and the Gannet are finishing theirs, repeat to me something more of Chivers!

THE ANCIENT. I can only recall fragments, here and there. The refrain to a poem called "The Poet's Vocation," in the "Eonchs of Ruby," is:—

> "In the music of the morns,
> Blown through the Conchimarian horns,
> Down the dark vistas of the reboantic Norns,
> To the Genius of Eternity,
> Crying: 'Come to me! Come to me!'"

ZOÏLUS. Ye gods! It is amazing. Why can't you write a stanza in his manner?

THE ANCIENT (*smiling*). I think I can even equal him.

(*He takes a pencil and writes rapidly. Just as he finishes,* GALAHAD *and* THE GANNET *lay down their pencils and lean back in their seats.*)

The Chorus (*eagerly*). We must first hear the Ancient! He is a medium for the great Chivers.

The Ancient. I have been merciful towards you. One stanza will suffice. (*Reads.*)

> Beloved of the wanderer's father
>   That walks mid the agates of June,
> The wreaths of remorse that I gather
>   Were torn from the turrets of Rune;
> When the star-patterns broidered so brilliant
>   Shone forth from the diapered blue,
> And the moon dropped her balsam scintilliant,
>   Soul-nectar for me and for you!

The Gannet. Send for a physician; tie a wet towel around his head! A thousand years hence, when the human race comes back to polytheism, Chivers will be the god of all crack-brained authors.

The Ancient. I recognize a fantastic infection. Come, Zoïlus, give me a tonic!

Zoïlus. Wine has become a very fashionable tonic, and that is just what I have put into Barry Cornwall's mouth. (*Reads.*)

SONG.

> Talk of dew on eglantine,—
> Stuff! the poet's drink is wine.
> Black as quaffed by old King Death,
> That which biteth, maddeneth;
> For my readers fain would see
> What effect it has on me.

Nose may redden, head may swim,
Joints be loose in every limb,
And the golden rhymes I chant
Sheer away on wings aslant,
Whale may whistle, porpoise roll,
Yet I'll drain the gentle bowl!

Pleasure's dolphin gambols near;
Virtue's mackerel looks austere;
Duty's hippopotamus
Waddles forward, leaving us;
Joy, the sturgeon, leaps and soars,
While we coast the Teian shores!

THE ANCIENT. What a fearful Bacchanalian you have made of good and gentle Barry Cornwall! You must have been possessed by Poe's "Imp of the Perverse," to yoke his manner to such a subject. I was expecting to hear something of spring and clover and cowslips. Faith! I believe I could improvise an imitation. Wait a second! Now:—

When spring returneth,
  And cowslips blow,
The milkmaid churneth
  Her creamy snow,
The mill-wheel spurneth
  The stream below;
The cherry-tree skippeth in earth and air,
The small bird calleth: beware, prepare!
And all is fair!

OMNES. Another stanza!

THE ANCIENT. O, you have but to turn things upside down, and there it is:—

>   The cold wind bloweth
>   O'er brake and burn,
>   The cream o'erfloweth
>   The tilted churn,
>   The mill-wheel sloweth,
>   And fails to turn;
>   The cherry-tree sheddeth her leaves in the fall,
>   The crow and the clamoring raven call,
>   And that is all!

But, seriously, Galahad, after what Zoïlus has done, I am a little afraid of the Gannet's work. Suppose he should make our beloved Whittier

> "Troll a careless tavern-catch
> Of Moll and Meg, and strange experiences
> Unmeet for ladies"?

GALAHAD (*earnestly*). Then I should withdraw from the Club.

THE GANNET. Prythee, peace, young hotspur! I'll agree to start with you for Massachusetts by to-morrow morning's express train, and lay before the poet what I've written. If he does n't laugh heartily, on reading it, I'll engage to come all the way back afoot.

THE ANCIENT. We can decide for him: read!

THE GANNET. It is a ballad of New England life which you shall hear. (*Reads.*)

THE BALLAD OF HIRAM HOVER.

>   Where the Moosatockmaguntic
>   Pours its waters in the Skuntic,
>   Met, along the forest-side,
>   Hiram Hover, Huldah Hyde.

She, a maiden fair and dapper,
He, a red-haired, stalwart trapper,
 Hunting beaver, mink, and skunk,
 In the woodlands of Squeedunk.

She, Pentucket's pensive daughter,
Walked beside the Skuntic water,
 Gathering, in her apron wet,
 Snakeroot, mint, and bouncing-bet.

"Why," he murmured, loath to leave her,
"Gather yarbs for chills and fever,
 When a lovyer, bold and true,
 Only waits to gather you?"

"Go," she answered, "I'm not hasty;
I prefer a man more tasty:
 Leastways, one to please me well
 Should not have a beasty smell."

"Haughty Huldah!" Hiram answered;
"Mind and heart alike are cancered:
 Jest look here! these peltries give
 Cash, wherefrom a pair may live.

"I, you think, am but a vagrant,
Trapping beasts by no means fragrant;
 Yet — I'm sure it's worth a thank —
 I've a handsome sum in bank."

Turned and vanished Hiram Hover;
And, before the year was over,
 Huldah, with the yarbs she sold,
 Bought a cape, against the cold.

Black and thick the furry cape was;
Of a stylish cut the shape was;
    And the girls, in all the town,
    Envied Huldah up and down.

Then, at last, one winter morning,
Hiram came, without a warning:
    "Either," said he, " you are blind,
    Huldah, or you 've changed your mind.

"Me you snub for trapping varmints,
Yet you take the skins for garments:
    Since you wear the skunk and mink,
    There 's no harm in me, I think."

"Well," said she, " we will not quarrel,
Hiram: I accept the moral.
    Now the fashion 's so, I guess
    I can't hardly do no less."

Thus the trouble all was over
Of the love of Hiram Hover;
    Thus he made sweet Huldah Hyde
    Huldah Hover, as his bride.

Love employs, with equal favor,
Things of good and evil savor;
    That, which first appeared to part,
    Warmed, at last, the maiden's heart.

Under one impartial banner,
Life, the hunter, Love, the tanner,
    Draw, from every beast they snare,
    Comfort for a wedded pair!

ZoïLUS. The Gannet distances us all to-night. Even Galahad is laughing yet, and I saw, when the reading began, that he was resolved not to smile, if he could help it. What does our Ancient think?

THE ANCIENT. It does, certainly, suggest the style of some of Whittier's delightful ballads, only substituting a comical for an earnest motive. Change that motive and a few expressions, and it would become a serious poem. The Gannet was lucky in striking the proper key at the start. And here, perhaps, is one result of our diversions, upon which we had not calculated, over and above the fun. I don't see why poets should not drill themselves in all that is technical, as well as painters, sculptors, opera-singers, or even orators. All the faculties called into play to produce rhythm, harmony of words, richness of the poetical dialect, choice of keys and cadences, may be made nimbler, more active, and more obedient to command, by even mechanical practice. I never rightly believed in the peculiar solemnity of the poet's gift; every singer should have a gay, sportive side to his nature. I am sure the young Shakespeare would have heartily joined in what we are here doing; the young Goethe, we know, did many a similar thing. He was a capital *improvvisatore;* and who knows how much of his mastery over all forms of poetry may not have come from just such gymnastics?

GALAHAD. Might not an aptness in representing the manner of others — like that of an actor who assumes a different character every night — indicate some lack of original force?

THE ANCIENT. The comparison is deceptive. An

actor's sole business is to assume other individualities. What we do is no more than every novelist does, in talking as a young girl, an old man, a saint, or a sinner. If anything of yourself is lost in the process, and you can't get it back again, why — let it go!

ZOÏLUS. You have it now, Galahad!

GALAHAD. Well, I'll cover my confusion by transferring myself into Dante Gabriel Rossetti. (*Reads.*)

CIMABUELLA.

I.

Fair-tinted cheeks, clear eyelids drawn
    In crescent curves above the light
Of eyes, whose dim, uncertain dawn
    Becomes not day : a forehead white
Beneath long yellow heaps of hair :
She is so strange she must be fair.

II.

Had she sharp, slant-wise wings outspread,
    She were an angel ; but she stands
With flat dead gold behind her head,
    And lilies in her long thin hands :
Her folded mantle, gathered in,
Falls to her feet as it were tin.

III.

Her nose is keen as pointed flame ;
    Her crimson lips no thing express ;
And never dread of saintly blame
    Held down her heavy eyelashés :

To guess what she were thinking of
Precludeth any meaner love.

IV.

An azure carpet, fringed with gold,
   Sprinkled with scarlet spots, I laid
Before her straight, cool feet unrolled:
   But she nor sound nor movement made
(Albeit I heard a soft, shy smile,
Printing her neck a moment's while);

V.

And I was shamed through all my mind
   For that she spake not, neither kissed,
But stared right past me. Lo! behind
   Me stood, in pink and amethyst,
Sword-girt and velvet-doubleted,
A tall, gaunt youth, with frowzy head,

VI.

Wide nostrils in the air, dull eyes,
   Thick lips that simpered, but, ah me!
I saw, with most forlorn surprise,
   He was the Thirteenth Century,
I but the Nineteenth; then despair
Curdled beneath my curling hair.

VII.

O, Love and Fate! How could she choose
   My rounded outlines, broader brain,
And my resuscitated Muse?
   Some tears she shed, but whether pain

Or joy in him unlocked their source,
I could not fathom which, of course.

VIII.

But I from missals, quaintly bound,
   With cither and with clavichord
Will sing her songs of sovran sound:
   Belike her pity will afford
Such faint return as suits a saint
So sweetly done in verse and paint.

THE GANNET. O Galahad! Who could have expected this of you?

GALAHAD. You know I like Rossetti's poems, but, really, I could n't help it, after I once got under way.

THE GANNET. Rossetti is picturesque, whatever else he may not be. His poetry has a delicate flavor of its own, and that is much to me, in these days, when so many dishes seem to be cooked with the same sauce. A poet is welcome to go back to the thirteenth century, if he only fetches us pictures. Poetry belongs to luxurious living, as much as painting and music; hence we must value color, rhythmical effect, quaint and unexpected play of fancy, and every other quality that makes verse bright and sparkling. The theme is of less importance. Take, for instance, Victor Hugo's *Orientales*.

ZOÏLUS. Pray, let us not open that discussion again! You know, already, how far I go with you, and just where Galahad and The Ancient stand. We should rather confine ourselves directly to the authors we imitate. Now, I think Rossetti's book on the Early Italian Poets better than his own poems. Perhaps it was the attempt to reproduce those poets in English which has given the mediæval coloring to his verse. We cannot undertake to say how much of the manner is natural, and how much assumed; for a thirteenth or even a second century nature may be born nowadays. But it is none the less out of harmony with our thought and feeling, and the encouragement of such a fashion in literature strikes me as being related to the Pre-Raphaelite hallucination in art. I should like to have the Ancient's opinion on this point.

The Ancient. Here is your other name, Galahad. (*Gives him a slip of paper.*) If there were not so much confusion of taste, Zoïlus, — such an uncertainty in regard to the unchanging standards of excellence, in literature and art, — I could answer you in a few words. We must judge these anachronistic developments (as they seem) by those which provoked them. A movement may be false in itself, yet made necessary by some antecedent illusion or inanity. If you want to leave port, almost any craft will answer. I might carry out the image, and add that we never can foresee what side-winds may come to force the vessel to some other shore than that for which she seems bound. I have carefully read Rossetti's book, as one of the many phenomena of the day. It seems to me that there is a genuine thread of native poetry in him, but so encumbered with the burden of color, sensuous expression, and mediæval imagery and drapery, that it often is nearly lost. What I have heard of the author explains to me the existence of the volume; but its immediate popularity is something which I should not have anticipated.

GALAHAD. I have written.

THE GANNET. Already? Who was it, then?

GALAHAD. A personal friend, whose poems I know by heart, — Thomas Bailey Aldrich. Therefore, I could n't well avoid violating our rule, for a special little rhyme popped into my head, and imitated myself. If Aldrich were not living in Boston, we should have him here with us to-night, and he would be quite ready to burlesque himself. (*Reads.*)

PALABRAS GRANDIOSAS.

I lay i' the bosom of the sun,
Under the roses dappled and dun.
I thought of the Sultan Gingerbeer,
In his palace beside the Bendemeer,
With his Affghan guards and his eunuchs blind,
And the harem that stretched for a league behind.
The tulips bent i' the summer breeze,
Under the broad chrysanthemum-trees,
And the minstrel, playing his culverin,
Made for mine ears a merry din.
If I were the Sultan, and he were I,
Here i' the grass he should loafing lie,
And I should bestride my zebra steed,
And ride to the hunt of the centipede:
While the pet of the harem, Dandeline,
Should fill me a crystal bucket of wine,
And the kislar aga, Up-to-Snuff,
Should wipe my mouth when I sighed, "Enough!"
And the gay court-poet, Fearfulbore,
Should sit in the hall when the hunt was o'er,

And chant me songs of silvery tone,
Not from Hafiz, but — mine own!

Ah, wee sweet love, beside me here,
I am not the Sultan Gingerbeer,
Nor you the odalisque Dandeline,
Yet I am yourn, and you are mine!

THE ANCIENT. There's a delicate, elusive quality about Aldrich's short lyrics, which I should think very difficult to catch. I have an indistinct recollection of poor George Arnold writing something.

ZOÏLUS. It was all about a mistake Aldrich made, years ago, in the color of a crocus. He call it *red*, and there may be red crocuses for aught I know; but yellow or orange is the conventional color. Of course we didn't let the occasion slip; we were all unmerciful towards each other. I remember I wrote something like this: —

I walked in the garden, ruffled with rain,
Through the blossoms of every hue;
And I saw the pink, with its yellow stain,
And the rose, with its bud of blue.

George Arnold's lines were: —

And all about the porphyry plates were strewn
The blue arbutus of the early June,
The crimson lemon and the purple yam,
And dainties brought from Seringapatam!

THE GANNET. They are better than yours. Well, I'm glad that Galahad has not confused our color, at least. I specially like Aldrich; for he is faithful to his talent, and gives us nothing that is not daintily polished and rounded. Some of his fragments remind me of Genoese filigree-work, there seems to be so much elaboration in a small compass; yet only sport, not labor, is suggested. He, also, has ceased to sing in the minor key; but I don't think he ever affected it much.

The Ancient (*earnestly*). I'm glad to hear it! O ye cheerful gods of all great poets, shall we never have an end of weeping and wailing and lamentation! Is the world nothing but a cavern of sorrow, and the individual life a couch of thorns? Must we have always bats, and never skylarks, in the air of poetry?

Zoïlus. Hear, hear! I have not seen the Ancient so roused this many a day.

The Ancient. The truth always excites.

Galahad. Before you put on your hats, let us have one more "lager." (*The glasses are filled.*) Now, to the health of all our young authors!

The Gannet. Here's to them heartily, — for that includes ourselves.

The Ancient. As the youngest, I return thanks.

[*Exeunt.*

NIGHT THE FOURTH.

ALL the members of the club were assembled, but the Ancient had not yet made his appearance. He was dining that evening, as it happened, with a wealthy banker, and there was no possibility of omitting one of the seventeen courses, or escaping before the coffee and *liqueurs*. As the oldest of the members, the duties of chairman were always conferred on him whenever a decision became necessary, and all assumed, as a matter of course, that the Diversions should be suspended until his arrival. But the conversation, meanwhile, settled upon him as its subject. Zoïlus and one of the Chorus were not as old acquaintances as the Gannet and Galahad, which circumstance led, after his nature had been genially discussed, to the following digression :—

Zoïlus (*to* The Gannet). I had not often met him familiarly, in this way, before. He is a good, mellow-natured companion, and not at all dogmatic, that is, in a direct way; but I can see the influence of his Boston associations. There is a great deal of external tact and propriety in that city. Now, *our* impetuous, keen, incisive atmosphere —

The Gannet (*interrupting*). Spare me the "incisive"! It has been overdone, as an effect, and will be the ruin of you, yet. If I had as much faith as Galahad there, I should believe as the Ancient does. But, since you will have the "incisive," where can you find sentences more clearly cut — the very intaglio of style — than in Holmes?

Zoïlus (*angrily*). And do you remember what he wrote of our New York authors, —

> "Whose fame, beyond their own abode,
> Extends — for miles along the Harlem road"?

The Gannet. Yes, and don't you know who they were? Why, their fame does n't reach up to Twenty-third Street, now! It was a deliberate attempt, by a small clique, to manufacture the Great American Literature. The materials were selected in advance, the style and manner settled, and then the great authors went to work. Like the Chinese mechanics who copied a steamboat, the external imitation was perfect; but there were no inside works, and it would n't move a paddle! When you speak of our legitimate authors, here in New York, what name first comes to your lips? Bryant, of course; and have you forgotten how Holmes celebrated him? and how his was the only garland of verse thrown upon Halleck's grave?

Zoïlus. Nevertheless, they systematically depreciate what we do; they are only kind and considerate towards one another. You remember Poe's experience?

The Ancient (*entering the room*). Which one, pray?

Zoïlus. Of Boston. But they did not and have not put *him* down!

The Ancient. Why, no; he put himself down, that time: I happened to be there, and I saw the performance. I guess that you and the Gannet have been repeating your usual tilt; why not say, as Goethe did of the comparisons made between himself and Schiller, "Instead of quarrelling about which of us is the greater, people ought simply to be thankful for having us both"? Thirty or forty years ago, when Lowell and Whipple were boys, Longfellow and Holmes young authors, Emerson considered little better than daft, and Whittier almost outlawed on account of his antislavery opinions, the literary society here included Irving, Cooper, Bryant, Willis, and Halleck, then the foremost American authors. The chief literary periodicals were here and in Philadelphia; and Boston, although the average of intellectual culture was always higher there than elsewhere, occupied quite a secondary place. But I don't remember that there was ever any jealousy or rivalry; and I confess I can't understand the spirit which fosters such a feeling now.

Zoïlus. You have passed the age when you care for recognition.

The Ancient. Have I, indeed? Pray, when does that age cease? If I had a more general recognition, at present,— by which I mean the ascription to me of exactly the literary qualities which I think I possess, — I should be stimulated to do more and possibly better work. I began authorship at a time when there was not much discrimination between varieties of literary talent, when such fearful stuff as "Agathé, a Necromaunt: in Three Chimæras," by a man named Tasistro, was published in "Graham's Magazine," and when a dentist in Rhode

Island wrote a poem in heroic verse, called "The Dentiad."

The Gannet. What was his name?

The Ancient. Solyman Brown. I must quote to you an exquisite passage: —

> "Whene'er along the ivory disks are seen
> The rapid traces of the dark gangrene,
> When caries come, with stealthy pace, to throw
> Corrosive ink-spots on those banks of snow,
> Brook no delay, ye trembling, suffering Fair,
> But fly for refuge to the dentist's care.
> His practised hand, obedient to his will,
> Employs the slender file with nicest skill;
> Just sweeps the germin of disease away,
> And stops the fearful progress of decay."

Zoïlus. The latest nursling of Darwin's "Botanic Garden"! It is not antithetical enough for Pope. Surely, that was not a popular poem?

The Ancient. I was too young to know. I only mention it as one of the chaotic elements out of which has grown what little permanent literature we now have. Probably three fourths of the writers then commencing their career might have developed some sound practical ability, with a little intelligent guidance; they were not strong enough to beat their own way out of the wilderness. When I look back upon the time, I can see the bones of immortal works bleaching on all sides.

The Gannet. As ours will bleach for the young fellows who sit here in 1900! While you were speaking, the thought occurred to me that no young poet in England can possibly be as green at his entrance into literature as the most of us must inevitably be. I begin to see that a conventional standard is better than none; for if it does not guide, it provokes resistance; either way, therefore, the neophyte acquires a definite form and style.

THE ANCIENT. To that extent, I agree with you. But we also have a standard, only those who accept it are fewer, and so scattered over the whole country that their authority is not immediately felt. They distinguish between what is temporary and what is permanent, in spite of the general public. And this ought to be our great comfort, if we are in earnest, that no power on earth can keep alive a sensational reputation.

ZOÏLUS. How do you account for the popularity of such single poems as "The River of Time," (is that the title of it?) and "Beautiful Snow," and "Rock me to sleep, Mother?" Why, hardly a week passes, but I see a newspaper dispute about the authorship of one or the other of them! To me they are languishing sentiment, not poetry.

THE ANCIENT. "Sentiment" sufficiently accounts for their popularity. Put some tender, thoroughly obvious sentiment into rhyme which sounds like the melody of a popular song, and it will go through hides which are impervious to the keenest arrows of the imagination. But how much more unfortunate for us, if it were not so! This gives us just the fulcrum we need if our literature is ever to be an Archimedean lever. I find myself a great deal happier since I have set about discovering the reason of these manifestations of immature taste, instead of lamenting over them, or cursing them, as I once did.

ZoÏlus (*ironically*). Then I have not attained your higher stand-point?

The Gannet (*offering him the hat*). Here, pick out one of the caged birds, and make him sing! The prelude of chords and discords has lasted long enough; let the orchestra now fall into a lively melody.

ZoÏlus. Ha! How shall I manage Bryant?

Galahad. Or I, Oliver Wendell Holmes?

The Gannet. Or I, N. P. Willis?

Galahad. Let us either exchange, or deal again!

The Ancient. No! As chairman, I declare such a proposition out of order. You must not pick out those authors with whose manner you are most familiar, or whom you could most easily imitate. That would be no fair and equal test; and there must be a little emulation, to keep your faculties in nimble playing condition. I am as oddly tasked as either of you, — see, I have drawn Tennyson! — yet, for the sake of good example, I'll work with you this time. Let us surrender ourselves, like spiritual mediums, to the control of the first stray idea that enters our brains: anything whatever will do for a point to start from. I am curious to know what will come of it.

ZoÏlus. So am I. Here goes. (*Writes.*)

The Gannet. We must first have our glasses filled; Galahad, ring for the waiter!

(*A silence of fifteen or twenty minutes follows. As the first one who has completed his task lifts his head with a sigh of relief, the others write with a nervous haste; but all wait for the last one.*)

The Gannet. You were ready first, ZoÏlus.

ZoÏLUS. Then it was not because I had the least difficult task. Perhaps our Ancient can tell me why it is so difficult to make an echo for Bryant's verse. To parody any particular poem, such as "The Death of the Flowers," would be easy enough, I should think; but I was obliged to write something independent in Bryant's manner. Now, when I asked myself, "What is his manner?" I could only answer, "Gravity of subject and treatment, pure rhythm, choice diction, and a mixture more or less strong of the moral element."

THE ANCIENT. You have fairly stated his prominent characteristics, and your difficulty came from the fact that they are all so evenly and exquisitely blended in his verse, that no single one seems salient enough to take hold of. Bryant's range of subjects is not wide, but within that range he is a most admirable artist. He is of the same blood with Wordsworth, — a brother, not a follower, — and oftentimes seems cold, because his intellectual pitch is high. I confess *I* find the powers of control, temperance, self-repression, abnegation of sentiment for a purpose which aims beyond it, in his poems, rather than a negative coldness. His literary position, it is true, is very isolated. He has both kept aloof from the temporary excitements in our poetic atmosphere, and he has rarely given any direct expression of an aspiration for the general literary development of our people, or of sympathy with those who felt and fostered it. Nevertheless, we cannot fairly go beyond an author's works, in our judgments; and I suspect we shall all agree, as Americans, in estimating the amount of our debt to Bryant.

GALAHAD. You have so put down my natural reverence that I don't dare to protest. But when I see Bryant in Broadway, with his magnificent Homeric beard, I wonder the people don't take off their hats as he passes. Why, seventy years ago, the stolid Berliners almost carried Schiller on their shoulders as he came out of the theatre; the raging mob of '48 did homage to Humboldt; and every other people, it seems to me, in every other civilized land, has rendered some sort of honor to its minstrels. But I cannot recollect that we have ever done anything.

The Gannet. Yes, we have done a little, but not much, — after death. A few men have given Halleck a monument, and two men have put up busts of Irving and Bryant in our parks. There was a public commemoration of Cooper, at which Webster (who knew nothing and cared nothing about our literature) officiated; but that was the end of it. The Bryant Festival was almost a private matter; the public was not represented, and one author belonging to the same club refused to take any part in it, on account of the political views of the poet!

The Ancient. We are forgetting our business. Zoïlus has the floor.

Zoïlus. I told you I had a hard task; therefore I shall not be vexed if you tell me I have failed. (*Reads.*)

THE DESERTED BARN.

Against the gray November sky,
  Beside the weedy lane, it stands;
To newer fields they all pass by,
  The farmers and their harvest hands.

There is no hay within the mow;
   The racks and mangers fall to dust;
The roof is crumbling in, but thou,
   My soul, inspect it and be just.

Once from the green and winding vale
   The sheaves were borne to deck its floor;
The blue-eyed milkmaid filled her pail,
   Then gently closed the stable door.

Once on the frosty winter air
   The sound of flails afar was borne,
And from his natural pulpit there
   The preacher cock called up the morn.

But all are gone: the harvest men
   Work elsewhere now for higher pay;
The blue-eyed milkmaid married Ben,
   The hand, and went to Ioway.

The flails are banished by machines,
   Which thrash the grain with equine power;
The senile cock no longer weans
   The folk from sleep at dawning hour.

They slumber late beyond the hill,
   In that new house which spurns the old;
In gorgeous stalls the kine are still,
   The horse is blanketed from cold.

But I from ostentatious pride
   And hollow pomp of riches turn,
To muse that ancient barn beside:
   Pause, pilgrim, and its lesson learn;

> So live, that thou shalt never make
>   A mill-pond of the mountain-tarn,
> Nor for a gaudy stable take
>   The timbers of thy ruined barn!

GALAHAD. I vow I don't know whether that is serious, or a burlesque imitation!

THE ANCIENT. Then Zoïlus has fairly succeeded. The grave, autumnal tone was indispensable, for it stamps itself on the minds of nine out of ten who read Bryant; just as we always associate Wordsworth with mountain walks and solitary musings. Did you ever see Kuntze's statuette of Bryant? He is sitting, and beside him, on the ground, there is only a buffalo-skull. Of course, you at once imagine a prairie mound, with nothing in sight, — which is carrying the impression altogether too far; for his poems on the apple-tree and the bobolink are entirely human.

GALAHAD (*earnestly*). There is much more than that in his poetry! There is the evidence of a high imaginative quality, which, for some reason or other, he seems to hold in check! Read "The Land of Dreams" and his poem on "Earth," where there is something about the

> "Hollows of the great invisible hills
>   Where darkness dwells all day —"

I can't remember all the passage, but it is exceedingly fine! Generally, he reins himself up so tightly that you cannot feel the fretting of the bit; but rarely, when he lets himself go, for a few lines, you get a glimpse of another nature.

THE ANCIENT. Just therein, I think, lies his greatest service to American literature. There have always been, and always will be, enough of wild mustangs, unbridled foals, who dash off at a gallop and can't stop themselves at the proper goal, but pant and stagger a mile beyond it. With Bryant's genius, he might have undertaken much more; but he has hoarded his power, and how freshly it serves him still!

> "No waning of fire, no quenching of ray,
> But rising, still rising, then passing away."

Who wrote those lines?

THE GANNET. He who speaks through me to-night, — Willis. But Galahad comes next in order.

GALAHAD. I have really a better right to complain of the severity of my task than Zoïlus. One can't imitate humor without possessing it, — which I 'm not sure that I do. Between "Old Ironsides" and the "One-Hoss Shay," Holmes has played in a great many keys, and I was forced to echo that one which seemed easiest to follow. (*Reads.*)

THE PSYCHO-PHYSICAL MUSE.

O Muse, descend, or, stay! — evolve thy presence from within,
For all conditions now combine, and so I must begin:
The wind is fresh from west-nor'west, the sky is deepest blue,
Thermometer at seventy, and pulse at seventy-two.

At breakfast fish-balls I consumed; the phosphates are supplied!
The peccant acid in my blood by Selters alkalied;

As far as I can see the works, my old machine of thought
Runs with its cogs and pivots oiled, as if in Waltham bought.

The main-spring is elastic yet, the balance-wheel is trim,
And if "full-jewelled" one should think, let no man scoff at him!
Odi profanum vulgus, — well! the truth is t' other way;
But one eupeptic as myself can always have his say.

Suppose I let the wheels run on, till fancy's index-hand
Points to a verse-inspiring theme and there inclines to stand?
Between the thought and rhythmic speech there often yawns a chasm;
To bridge it o'er we only need a vigorous protoplasm.

With an unconscious sinciput, a cerebellum free,
I don't see why the loftiest lays should not be sung by me:
The fitful flushes of the Muse my diagnosis own:
I test her symptoms in the air as surely as ozone.

There's just one thing that fails me yet; the fancies dart around
Like skittish swallows on the wing, but none will touch the ground.
With such conditions 't were a sin to lay the pen aside,
But, with the mind close-girt to run, direction is denied.

I've waited, now, an hour or more: I'd take a glass of wine,
Save that I fear 't would send the pulse to seventy-eight or nine;
'T is that capricious jade, the Muse!—I know her tricks of old:
Just when my house is warm for her, she *will* prefer the cold!

THE GANNET. Ah, you've only caught some general characteristics, not the glitter and flash of Holmes's lines! His humor is like a Toledo blade; it may be sheathed in a circular scabbard, but it always springs out straight and keen, and fit for a direct lunge. He is the only poet in the country who can write good "occasionals," without losing faith in the finer inspiration, or ceasing to obey it.

GALAHAD. You very well know we have no time for selection. I have been reading lately his "Mechanism in Thought and Morals," so that my imitation was really suggested by his prose.

THE ANCIENT. That is permitted. For my part, though I like Holmes's songs in all keys, I have always wished that he had written more such poems as "La Grisette," wherein we have, first of all, ease and grace, then just enough of sentiment, of humor, and of a light, sportive fancy to make a mixture wholly delightful, — a beverage that cheers, but not inebriates, in which there is neither headache nor morbid tears. Hood had the same quality, though he does n't often reveal it; so had Praed; so, I feel sure, had Willis, but in his case it was a neglected talent. When I say that we most sorely need this naïve, playful element in our literature, you may not agree with me; but, O, how tired I am of hearing that every poem should "convey a lesson," should "inculcate a truth," should "appeal to the moral sense." Why, half our self-elected critics seem to be blind to the purely æsthetic character of our art! No man — not even the greatest — can breathe a particular atmosphere all his life, without taking some of its ingredients into his blood; and just those which seem best may be most fatal to the imaginative faculty. I suspect there has been more of battle in the intellectual life of Holmes than any of us knows.

Zoïlus. Now let us hear the Gannet.

The Gannet. If it had been a leader for the "Home Journal," I should have found the task light enough; but Willis's poetic style is — as he would have said — rather un-come-at-able. (*Reads.*)

KEREN-HAPPUCH.

The comforters of Job had come and gone.
They were anhungered; for the eventide
Sank over Babylon, and smokes arose
From pottage cooked in palace and in tent.
Then Keren-happuch, from her lordly bower
Of gem-like jasper, and the porphyry floors
Swept by the satins of her trailing robe,
Came forth, and sat beside her father Job,
And gave him comfort, mid his painful boils,
And scraped him with a potsherd; and her soul
Rebelled at his unlovely misery,
And from her lips, that parted like a cleft
Of ripe pomegranates o'er their ruby teeth,
Broke forth a wail:

" Alas for thee, my sire!
And for the men and maidens of thy train,
And for thy countless camels on the plain,
   More than thou didst require;
Thou mightst have sold them at the morning dawn
For heavy gold: at even they were gone!

" And they who dressed my hair
With agate braids and pearls from Samarcand

Have died; there is no handmaid in the land,
        To make my visage fair:
Unpainted and unpowdered, lo! I come,
Gray with the ashes of my gorgeous home!

"Yea, thou and I are lone:
The prince who wooed me fled in haste away
From thine infection: hungered here I stray,
        And find not any bone;
For famished cats have ravaged shelf and plate:
The larder, like my heart, is desolate!

"And it is very drear,
My sire, whose wealth and beauty were my pride,
To see thee so disfigured at my side,
        Nor leech nor poultice near,
To save thy regal skin from later scars:
Yea, thou art loathsome by the light of stars!

"Go, hie thee to thy room,
And I will gather marjoram and nard,
And mix their fragrance with the cooling lard,
        And thus avert thy doom.
A daughter's sacrifice no tongue can tell:
The prince will not return till thou art well!"

GALAHAD. Now I must say, although I have enjoyed the travesty with you, that this gives me a pang. I can't forget Willis's sunny, kindly, and sympathetic nature, and the dreary clouding of his mind at the last. There was something very tragic in the way in which he clung to the fragments that remained, as one faculty after another failed him, and strove to be still the cheerful, sparkling author of old. I was hardly more than a boy when I first went to him, a few years ago, and no brother could have been kinder to me.

The Ancient. There never was a poet more free from jealousy or petty rivalry, none more ready to help or encourage. As an author, he was damaged by too early popularity, and he made the mistake of trying to retain it through exaggerating the features of his style which made him popular; but neither homage nor defamation — and he received both in full measure — ever affected the man's heart in his breast. There was often an affectation of aristocratic elegance in his writings; yet, in his life, he was as natural a democrat as Walt Whitman, gentle, considerate, and familiar with the lowest whom he met, and only haughty towards ignorant or vulgar pretension. Poe said that he narrowly missed placing himself at the head of American literature, which was true of his career from 1830 to about 1845. By the by, I wish some one would undertake to write our literary history, beginning, say, about 1800.

Zoïlus. Set about it yourself! But, come, we are not to be cheated out of your contribution to-night; where is your Tennyson?

The Ancient. I have added another to his brief modern idyls. (*Reads.*)

EUSTACE GREEN;

Or, The Medicine-Bottle.

Here's the right place for lunch; and if, ah me!
The hollies prick, and burr-weed grows too near,
We'll air our eyesight o'er the swelling downs,

And so not mind them.   While the Medoc chills
In ice, and yon champagne-flask in the sun
Takes mellower warmth, I'll tell you what I did
To Eustace Green — last Cambridge-term it was,
Just when the snowball by the farmer's gate
Made jokes of winter at the garden rose.

No marvel of much wisdom Eustace was, —
You know him, Hal, — no high-browed intellect,
Such as with easy grab the wrangler's place
Plucks from the clutching hands of college youth,
But home-bred, as it were ; and all the stock,
His stalwart dad, and mother Marigold
(We called her), Kate, Cornelia, Joseph, Jane,
A country posy of great boys and girls.
But she, the mother, when the brown ash took
A livelier green beside the meadow-stile,
And celandines, the milky kine of flowers,
Were yellow in the lanes, hung o'er the fire
A caldron huge — oh me, it was a sight
To see her stir the many herbs therein !
Of yarrow, tansy, thyme, and camomile —
What know I all ? — she boiled and slowly brewed
The strange concoction : 't was an heirloom old,
The recipe, a sovran cure, and famed
From Hants to Yorkshire : this must Eustace take.
Not that the lubber lad was ill — O, no !
You did but need to punch him in the ribs,
To feel how muscle overlaid the bone ;
And as for trencher-practice, — trust me, Hal,
A donkey-load of lunch were none too much,
Were he here with us.   Where was I ? — Ah, yes,
The medicine !   She gave it me with words

Many, and thrice repeated ; he should take,
Eustace, the dose at morn, and noon, and night,
For these were feverous times : she did not know,
Not she, what airs blew o'er the meads of Cam :
Preventive ounces weighed a pound of cure.
At last, I thrust the bottle in my sack,
And left her.
    Now, returning Cambridge-wards,
Some devil tickled me to turn the thing
To joke, or was it humors in the blood,
Stirring, perchance, when, oysters out of date
And game prohibited, the stomach pines?
Think as you will ; but to myself my mind
Thus reasoned : need to him of medicine
Is none : the green cicala in the grass
Chirps not more wholesome : wherefore swiftly I
Will cast this useless brewage to the winds,
Yea, to the thistled downs ; and substitute —
Haply some ancient hostel glimmering near —
Laborious Boreal brandy, equal bulk.
And this, the thing accomplished, then did I
Proffer to Eustace Green, all eager he
For news of home and mother Marigold,
His dad and Kate, Cornelia, Joseph, Jane,
And Bloss, the ox, and Bounce, the plough-horse old,
One-eyed, and spavined. But the medicine
He took with : " Pshaw ! that beastly stuff again ?
Am I a rat that she should send the dose ? "
Then I : " Dear Eustace, times are feverous :
Malarial breezes blow across the Cam :
Preventive ounces weigh a pound of cure."
" O, damn your ounces ! " he profanely cried ;
" But if I must, I must ; so summon Giles,

The undertaker, when I take this dose,
And gently coffin me when now I die."
So drank; and then, with great eyes all astare,
Cried: "Taste it, you! Fourth-proof, O. P. and S. T. X.!—
We 'll have a puuch!" And that teetotal dame,
His mother, did we pledge in steaming punch,
She knowing not; and tears of laughter ran
Down both our cheeks, and trickled in the bowl,
Weakening the punch.
     But now the Medoc's chill,
And warm the sweet champagne; so, while the copse
Clangs round us like the clang of many shields,
Down the long hollows to the dusky sea,
Let us, with sandwich and the hard-boiled egg,
Enjoy both nature's beauty and our own!

OMNES. Well done!

ZOÏLUS. Why, you have caught the very trick of Tennyson's blank-verse! If you had only warmed the Medoc and chilled the champagne, I should hardly know the difference. But how did you ever happen to invent a motive, or plot, all complete, on the spur of the moment?

THE ANCIENT. Ah, you force me to confess: I did n't invent it. It was a trick I played myself, on a friend, in our young days; and, by good luck, it came to my memory just at the right time. Therefore, having the subject, the imitation of Tennyson's manner was easy enough. I 'm glad, however, that you think it successful; for it justifies me in holding fast to the principle we accepted, and which I was obliged to enforce to-night. You know that my own scattering poems are quite unlike — however long the interval between — anything of Tennyson's; but I have made it a point, for years past, to study the individual characteristics of the poets, and this proves how easily those which are superficial and obvious may be copied.

ZOÏLUS. May I ask what your private estimate of Tennyson, as a poet, is?

THE ANCIENT. Of course! While I might, possibly, agree with his keenest critics in regard to many details of style or expression, especially in his earlier poems, I yield to no one in the profoundest respect for his noble loyalty to his art. Tennyson is a poet, who, recognizing the exact quality of his gift, has given all the forces of his mind, all the energies of his life, to perfect it. I can see that he has allowed no form of knowledge, which this age has developed, to arise without assimilating, at least, its substance; but all is employed in the sole service of his poetic art. He began with something of the rank, "lush" luxuriance of style which Keats was just leaving behind him when he died: he now rises, often to a majestic simplicity and dignity which nearly remind me of Milton. Not that the two are similar, in any particular; but Tennyson, like scarcely any other except Schiller, has achieved high success as a poet by comprehending clearly both his powers and their limitations. How easily, by mistaking his true work, he might have scattered his rays, instead of gathering them into a clear focus of light! All honor to him, I say, in this age, when so many writers degrade their gift by making it subservient to worldly ends!

GALAHAD (*with enthusiasm*). You make me happy!

The Gannet. I should say, nevertheless, that he was well paid in ringing guineas. For instance —

Zoïlus. "The continuation in next week's New York Ledger!" Do you know that it is one o'clock?

Omnes (*starting up*). We go — but we return!

[*Exeunt.*

NIGHT THE FIFTH.

LL were on hand at the usual hour, fresh and eager for a continuation of the performances. The Gannet, addressing Zoïlus, opened the conversation: —

"I can guess one thing you have been thinking of since we met, — of Tennyson's place in literature?"

ZOÏLUS. You have just hit it! I did n't fully agree with the Ancient, but there was no time left for discussion. There must be some good reason for Tennyson's influence on the poetry of our day; yet, if his is a genuine flower, it could n't be made a weed by being sown everywhere. There is no doubt of the individuality of his manner, but I am not yet ready to say that it is pure, as Collins's, or Gray's, for instance, or even Wordsworth's. He is sometimes like a perfume which cloys the sense from over-richness. Now, a very slight change in the odor of the tuberose might make it unpleasant; and it seems to me that some of Tennyson's younger followers have made just such a change.

GALAHAD. Almost the same thought occurred to me the other day. I was trying to recall some lines of the Ancient's imitation, and then went over in my mind the numbers of blank-verse idyls more or less in Tennyson's manner, which have been written by others. He drew from a very far source, as I think Stedman has clearly shown in his paper on "Theocritus and Tennyson"; but they, drawing from him, cannot conceal theirs. I never before felt so keenly the difference between the poetry which rises out of a man's own nature and that which is impressed upon it, or communicated, like an infection, by another mind. I even went so far as to try my hand alone, on an imitation of this idyllic school, which I now see is itself an echo.

The Ancient. Read it to us, then! Who was your immediate model?

Galahad (*taking a paper from his pocket*). Why, no one in particular. Now, that I look over the lines, I see that I must have been thinking of the echoes of the "Princess," rather than of those of the short idyls of modern life. It is the craziest burlesque of the mediæval themes, revived in that form: it is absurd, and nothing else.

Zoïlus. That will do very well, for variety.

Galahad. Then, as Eustace Green says, if I must, I must. (*Reads.*)

SIR EGGNOGG.

Forth from the purple battlements he fared,
Sir Eggnogg of the Rampant Lily, named
From that embrasure of his argent shield
Given by a thousand leagues of heraldry
On snuffy parchments drawn, — so forth he fared,
By bosky boles and autumn leaves he fared,

Where grew the juniper with berries black,
The sphery mansions of the future gin.
But naught of this decoyed his mind, so bent
On fair Miasma, Saxon-blooded girl,
Who laughed his loving lullabies to scorn,
And would have snatched his hero-sword to deck
Her haughty brow, or warm her hands withal,
So scornful she: and thence Sir Eggnogg cursed
Between his teeth, and chewed his iron boots
In spleen of love. But ere the morn was high
In the robustious heaven, the postern-tower
Clang to the harsh, discordant, slivering scream
Of the tire-woman, at the window bent
To dress her crispéd hair. She saw, ah woe!
The fair Miasma, overbalanced, hurled
O'er the flamboyant parapet which ridged
The muffled coping of the castle's peak,
Prone on the ivory pavement of the court,
Which caught and cleft her fairest skull, and sent
Her rosy brains to fleck the Orient floor.
This saw Sir Eggnogg, in his stirrups poised,
Saw he and cursed, with many a deep-mouthed oath,
And, finding nothing more could reunite
The splintered form of fair Miasma, rode
On his careering palfrey to the wars,
And there found death, another death than hers.

ZOÏLUS. After this, write another such idyl yourself, if you dare!

GALAHAD. I never shall; but when you have done the thing ignorantly, and a magazine wants it on account of the temporary popularity of the theme and manner, is an author much to blame for publishing?

The Gannet. Let your conscience rest, Galahad! "Hunger and request of friends" were always valid pleas. If a poet invariably asked himself, "Is this original? Is it something that *must* be written? Is it likely to be immortal?" I suspect our stock of verse would soon be very short. At least, only the Chiverses and Tuppers and —— would still be fruitful.

The Ancient. Did you ever guess at the probable permanence of the things which seem best when they appear? It is a wholesome experiment. Macaulay first suggested it to me, in speaking of the three per cent of Southey which might survive: since then, I have found that the Middle Ages are an immense graveyard of poems, but nothing to what this century will be. I doubt whether many authors would write, in the mere hope of posthumous fame.

The Gannet. *I* would n't! My idea of literature is, the possession of a power which you can wield to some purpose while you live. It may also be wealth, another power; it may be yoked with politics, which is better still; it may —

Galahad (*interrupting*). Stop! don't make me feel that your gift, which I have believed in, is so entirely selfish!

Zoïlus (*shaking the hat*). Here would soon be a precious row between you two; draw your names and go to work!

The Gannet. What? Henry T. Tuckerman?

Zoïlus. To be sure! I have — Longfellow!

Galahad. Mine is William D. Howells.

The Ancient. I have drawn Richard Henry Stoddard. Now, no changing, remember! We are better suited than the last time, unless it be Zoïlus, of whom I have my doubts. All imitations cannot be equally fortunate, and I'm not sure that any of us would succeed better, if he should take his own time and pains for the task, instead of trusting to the first random suggestion.

Zoïlus. Then, why are you doubtful about me? I have my random suggestion already.

The Ancient. Work it out! I think you understand my doubt, nevertheless. The Gannet is chuckling to himself, as if he were on the track of something wicked: I foresee that I must use my authority to-night, if I have any left. (*Writes.*)

The Chorus (*whispering together*). They are very evenly matched. Could any inference be drawn from the manner of each, as he writes? The Gannet has the most sarcastic air, Zoïlus is evidently satisfied with his performance, Galahad seems earnest and a little perplexed, and the Ancient is cool and business-like. They have all learned something by practice; they work much more rapidly than at first.

The Gannet (*after all have finished*). When you try to grasp anything smooth, your hand slips. In Tuckerman there is only proper smoothness which can be travestied, and you know how difficult that is. (*Reads.*)

ODE TO PROPRIETY.

Thou calm, complacent goddess of the mind,
  Look on me from thine undisturbed domain;
Thy well-adjusted leaflets let me bind,
  As once on youthful, now on manly brain.

Upon thy head there is no hair awry;
 Thy careful drapery falleth as it should:
Thy face is grave; thy scrutinizing eye
 Sees only that which hath been stamped as good.

Thou art no patron of the strenuous thought
 That speaks at will, regardless of old rule;
To thee no neologic lays are brought,
 But models of the strictly classic school.

Thou teachest me the proper way and sure;
 To no imaginative heights misled,
My verse moves onward with a step secure,
 Nor hastes with rapture, nor delays with dread.

I do not need to woo the fickle Muse,
 But am her master, justified by thee:
All measures must obey me as I choose,
 So long as they are thine, Propriety!

For genius is a fever of the blood,
 And lyric rage a strange, disturbing spell:
Let fools attempt the torrent and the flood,
 Beside the pensive, placid pond I dwell!

ZoïLUS. You have too much alliteration in the last line: that is not at all proper.

THE GANNET. Then it shows the impossibility of reproducing the tone of Pope and Gray in our day. I do not know that Tuckerman attempts this in his verse; but I suspect that his prose model is still Addison.

ZoïLUS. That is really getting to be a sign of originality! Mix Addison and Imagination together, and sublimate in a French retort, and where could you have a finer modern style? Tuckerman has all tradition on his side; he represents a conservative element in literature, which — though I don't admire it much — I think necessary, to keep the wild modern schools in order.

GALAHAD. It is something new, to hear you take this side.

ZOÏLUS. You must not always credit me with being wholly in earnest. I think I am a natural iconoclast; but one might as well assail respectability in society as the "classic" spirit in literature. It is impervious to all our shots; every blow slides off its cold polish. But, candidly, there are times when it seems to refresh me, or, at least, to give me a new relish for something warmer and more pungent.

THE ANCIENT. I believe you, fully. We should all fare badly, were it not for the colder works which we hear so often depreciated. They make a fire-proof temple in which we may build fires at will. Now, let us hear how you have treated an author who is already a classic, though without the *cold* polish of which you speak. Very few poets have been complimented by so many ordinary parodies.

ZOÏLUS. I am aware of that, and I have tried to get as far away as possible from the risk of resembling them. (*Reads.*)

NAUVOO.

This is the place: be still for a while, my high-pressure steam-
    boat!
Let me survey the spot where the Mormons builded their temple.
Much have I mused on the wreck and ruin of ancient religions,

Scandinavian, Greek, Assyrian, Zend, and the Sanskrit,
Yea, and explored the mysteries hidden in Talmudic targums,
Caught the gleam of Chrysaor's sword and occulted Orion,
Backward spelled the lines of the Hebrew graveyard at Newport,
Studied Ojibwa symbols and those of the Quarry of Pipe-stone,
Also the myths of the Zulus whose questions converted Colenso,
So, methinks, it were well I should muse a little at Nauvoo.

Fair was he not, the primitive Prophet, nor he who succeeded,
Hardly for poetry fit, though using the Urim and Thummim.
Had he but borrowed Levitical trappings, the girdle and ephod,
Fine-twined linen, and ouches of gold, and bells and pomegran-
      ates,
That, indeed, might have kindled the weird necromancy of fancy.
Had he but set up mystical forms, like Astarte or Peor,
Balder, or Freya, Quetzalcoatl, Perun, Manabozho,
Verily, though to the sense theologic it might be offensive,
Great were the gain to the pictured, flashing speech of the poet.
Yet the Muse that delights in Mesopotamian numbers,
Vague and vast as the roar of the wind in a forest of pine-trees,
Now must tune her strings to the names of Joseph and Brigham.
Hebrew, the first; and a Smith before the Deluge was Tubal,
Thor of the East, who first made iron ring to the hammer;
So on the iron heads of the people about him, the latter,
Striking the sparks of belief and forging their faith in the Good
      Time
Coming, the Latter Day, as he called it, — the Kingdom of Zion.
Then, in the words of Philip the Eunuch unto Belshazzar,
Came to him multitudes wan, diseased and decrepit of spirit,
Came and heard and believed, and builded the temple at Nauvoo.

All is past; for Joseph was smitten with lead from a pistol,
Brigham went with the others over the prairies to Salt Lake.

Answers now to the long, disconsolate wail of the steamer,
Hoarse, inarticulate, shrill, the rolling and bounding of ten-
    pins, —
Answers the voice of the bar-tender, mixing the smash and the
    julep,
Answers, precocious, the boy, and bites a chew of tobacco.
Lone as the towers of Afrasiab now is the seat of the Prophet,
Mournful, inspiring to verse, though seeming utterly vulgar:
Also — for each thing now is expected to furnish a moral —
Teaching innumerable lessons for whoso believes and is patient.
Thou, that readest, be resolute, learn to be strong and to suffer!
Let the dead Past bury its dead and act in the Present!
Bear a banner of strange devices, "Forever" and "Never"!
Build in the walls of time the fane of a permanent Nauvoo,
So that thy brethren may see it and say, "Go thou and do like-
    wise!"

GALAHAD. Zoïlus, you are incorrigible.

ZOÏLUS (*laughing*). Just what I expected you to say! But it's no easy thing to be funny in hexameters: the Sapphic verse is much more practicable. I heaped together everything I could remember, to increase my chances. In some of Longfellow's earlier poems the theme and moral are like two sides of a medal; but I could n't well copy that peculiarity.

THE GANNET. You will only find it in "The Beleaguered City" and "Seaweed." Longfellow is too genuine an artist to fall into that or any other "peculiarity." Just his best, his most purely imaginative poems are those which have not been popular, because the reader must be half a poet to appreciate them. What do you consider his best work?

Zoïlus. "Evangeline," of course.

The Gannet. No, it is the "Golden Legend"! That is the spirit of the Middle Ages, and the feeling of all ages, set to modern melodies. I think I could write an imitation of Longfellow's higher strains — not of those which are so well known and so much quoted — which would be fairer than yours.

Zoïlus. Do it, and good luck to you. (The Gannet *writes.*)

The Ancient. Not one of our poets has deserved better of his countrymen than Longfellow: he has advanced the front rank of our culture. His popularity has naturally brought envy and disparagement upon him; but it has carried far and wide among the people the influence of his purity, his refinement, and his constant reference to an ideal of life which so many might otherwise forget. As a nation, we are still full of crudity and confusion, and his influence, so sweet and clear and steady, has been, and is, more than a merely poetic leaven.

Galahad. I have felt that, without ever thinking of putting it into words. The sweetness of Longfellow's verse is its most *necessary* quality, when we consider his literary career in this light; but I never could see how exquisite finish implies any lack of power. What was that line of Goethe which you quoted to me once, Ancient?

The Ancient. *Nur aus vollendeter Kraft blicket die Anmuth hervor,* — only perfected Strength discloses Grace. There are singular ideas in regard to "power" afloat in literary circles. Why, the sunbeam is more powerful than a thousand earthquakes! I judge the power of an author by the influence of his works.

ZoÏlus. Well, for my part, I don't appreciate "power," unless it strikes me square between the eyes. What I understand by "power" is something regardless of elegance, of the conventional ideas of refinement, of what you call "laws of art," — something primitive, lawless, forcing you, with a strong hand, to recognize its existence.

The Ancient. Give me a few instances!

Zoïlus (*after a pause*). Carlyle, — Poe, — Swinburne, — Emily Brontë's "Wuthering Heights"!

Galahad. Why not Artemus Ward and Joaquin Miller?

The Gannet. There! I never quite succeed when I assume a certain ability. I had in my mind, Zoïlus, the "Prometheus and Epimetheus," the "Palingenesis," and other poems in the same key; but it was so difficult to imitate them that I came down one grade and struck into a style more easy to be recognized. It may not be better than yours, but it is not so horribly coarse. (*Reads.*)

THE SEWING-MACHINE.

A strange vibration from the cottage window
    My vagrant steps delayed,
And half abstracted, like an ancient Hindoo,
    I paused beneath the shade.

What is, I said, this unremitted humming,
    Louder than bees in spring?
As unto prayer the murmurous answer coming,
    Shed from Sandalphon's wing.

Is this the sound of unimpeded labor,
    That now usurpeth play?

Our harsher substitute for pipe and tabor,
    Ghittern and virelay?

Or, is it yearning for a higher vision,
    By spiritual hearing heard?
Nearer I drew, to listen with precision,
    Deciphering not a word.

Then, peering through the pane, as men of sin do,
    Myself the while unseen,
I marked a maiden seated by the window,
    Sewing with a machine.

Her gentle foot propelled the tireless treadle,
    Her gentle hand the seam:
My fancy said, it were a bliss to peddle
    Those shirts, as in a dream!

Her lovely fingers lent to yoke and collar
    Some imperceptible taste;
The rural swain, who buys it for a dollar,
    By beauty is embraced.

O fairer aspect of the common mission!
    Only the Poet sees
The true significance, the high position
    Of such small things as these.

Not now doth Toil, a brutal Boanerges,
    Deform the maiden's hand;
Her implement its soft sonata merges
    In songs of sea and land.

>And thus the hum of the unspooling cotton,
> Blent with her rhythmic tread,
>Shall still be heard, when virelays are forgotten,
> And troubadours are dead.

ZoïLUS. Ah, you could n't avoid the moral application!

THE ANCIENT. Neither can you, in imitating Bryant and Whittier. In Longfellow — excepting some half-dozen of his earlier poems — the moral element is so skilfully interfused with the imaginative, that one hardly suspects its presence. I should say, rather, that it is an inherent quality of his genius, and, therefore, can never offend like an assumed purpose. I abominate as much as you, Zoïlus, possibly can, the deliberate intention to preach moral doctrines in poetry. *That* is turning the glorious guild of authors into a higher kind of Tract Society! But the purer the poetic art, the nearer it approaches the loftiest morality; this is a truth which Longfellow illustrates. I have always defended the New England spirit against your prejudices, but this I must admit, that there is a large class of second-rate writers there who insist that every wayward little brook, whose murmur and sparkle are reason enough for its existence, must be made to turn some utilitarian mill. Over and over again, I have seen how their literary estimate of our poets is gauged by the assumed relation of the latter to some variety of "Reform." The Abolition of Slavery, first, then Temperance, and now Woman Suffrage, or Spiritualism, or the Labor Question, are dragged by the head and heels into the temple, and sometimes laid upon the very altar, of Letters. The wonder is, that this practice does n't retrospectively affect their judgment, and send Dante and Shakespeare and Milton to their chaotic limbo!

ZOÏLUS. Thanks for that much support; but let us hear Galahad!

GALAHAD. Howells, at least, has escaped some of the troubles through which the older authors have been obliged to pass. His four years in Venice made a fortunate separation between his youthful period and his true sphere of activity. He did not change front, as the rest of us must do, in the press of battle. I was very much puzzled what to select, as specially distinctive, and allowed myself, at last, to be guided by two or three short poems. (*Reads.*)

PREVARICATION.

. . . . .

THE ANCIENT. I think I know what you had in your mind. But I was expecting to hear something in hexameters: you know his — . . . . *

ZOÏLUS. Yes, but . . . .

GALAHAD. It is true to some extent. Still, on the other hand, he . . . .

---

* Mr. Howells, as Editor of the "Atlantic Monthly," insisted that he could not properly allow his name to appear among the poets. I did not agree with him; but I finally compromised our difference by omitting the travesty and the opinions, and adding foot-notes apparently written by himself. The latter were accepted as genuine and commented upon, to our mutual amusement. The imitation has been lost, or I should restore it now. — B. T.

Zoïlus. Well, after all, we seem to agree tolerably well. All our younger poets are tending towards greater finish and elegance. It is about time to expect the appearance of a third generation, with all the beauties and faults of their new youth about them. Why, we have hardly any known writer much less than thirty-five years old! Our lights scarcely begin to burn until the age when Keats's, Shelley's, Byron's, and Burns's went out. Is there something in our atmosphere that hinders development? I always supposed it possessed a greater stimulus.

The Ancient. If you look back a little, you will find that Bryant, Willis, Longfellow, and Lowell were known and popular authors at twenty-five. But I have noticed the lack of a younger generation of poets. It is equally true of England, France, and Germany; none of those who have made a strong impression, whether good or bad, can be called young, with the single exception of Swinburne. Rossetti, though he has appeared so recently, must be forty-five years old; and in Germany the most popular poets — Geibel, Bodenstedt, Hamerling, and Redwitz — are all in middle age. I think a careful study of the literary history of the last hundred years would show that we have had both the heroes and the *epigonoi*; and now nature requires a little rest. Of course, all theories on the subject must be merely fanciful; half a dozen young fellows of the highest promise may turn up in a month; but I rather expect to see a good many fallow years.

Galahad. Then I, at least, have fallen on evil times. If I live after our stars have set, and no new ones have arisen, it will be —

ZOÏLUS. Your great luck! *Parmi les aveugles*, you know; but we are forgetting the Ancient's imitation.

THE ANCIENT. Stoddard's last volume shows both variety and inequality, but the most of it has the true ring. I was delighted with his gift of poetic narration, in "The Wine-Cup" and "The King's Sentinel"; yet, even in them, there in an undertone of sadness. One can only make a recognizable echo of his verse, in the minor key. (*Reads.*)

THE CANTELOPE.

Side by side in the crowded street,
    Amid its ebb and flow,
We walked together one autumn morn;
    ('T was many years ago!)

The markets blushed with fruits and flowers;
    (Both Memory and Hope!)
You stopped and bought me at the stall
    A spicy cantelope.

We drained together its honeyed wine,
    We cast the seeds away;
I slipped and fell on the moony rinds,
    And you took me home on a dray!

The honeyed wine of your love is drained;
    I limp from the fall I had;
The snow-flakes muffle the empty stall,
    And everything is sad.

The sky is an inkstand, upside down,
    It splashes the world with gloom;

> The earth is full of skeleton bones,
>   And the sea is a wobbling tomb!

ZOÏLUS. I might have written that; what do you say, Galahad?

GALAHAD. It is fully as rollicking as yours, but not quite so coarse. I always find in Stoddard a most true and delicate ear for the melody of verse, and I thoroughly enjoy his brief snatches, or "catches," of song. When I disagree with him, it is usually on account of the theme rather than the execution. His collection of "Melodies and Madrigals" gave me the key to his own taste and talent; he seems to have wandered down to us from the times of Charles I. What has the Gannet been writing all this while?

THE GANNET. Something not on our programme. After trying my hand on Tuckerman and then on Longfellow, I felt fresh for one task more; and we have had so few ladies introduced into our diversions, that I turned to Mrs. Stoddard for a new inspiration. You know how I like her poems, as the efforts of a not purely rhythmic mind to express itself rhythmically. They interest me greatly, as every embodiment of struggle does. A commonplace, conventional intellect would never dare to do the things she does, both in prose and verse; she defies the usual ways to popularity with a most indomitable perseverance.

GALAHAD. Is not that the way to reach it in the end?

THE GANNET. No man knoweth; because no one can foresee how the tastes or whims of the mercurial public may turn. Some authors predict their own popularity;

some secretly expect it, and never get it; and some, again, leave works which may seem dead and buried, but are dug up as if by accident, after two or three centuries, and become new and delightful to a different race of men. Shall I read you my imitation?

THE ANCIENT. We wait.

THE GANNET. (*Reads.*)

THE NETTLE.

If days were nights, I could their weight endure.
This darkness cannot hide from me the plant
I seek: I know it by the rasping touch.
The moon is wrapped in bombazine of cloud;
The capes project like crooked lobster-shears
Into the bobbery of the waves; the marsh,
At ebb, has now a miserable smell.
I will not be delayed nor hustled back,
Though every wind should muss my outspread hair.
I snatch the plant that seems my coming fate:
I pass the crinkled satin of the rose,
The violets, frightened out of all their wits,
And other flowers, to me so commonplace,
And cursed with showy mediocrity,
To cull the foliage which repels and stings.
Weak hands may bleed; but mine are tough with pride,
And I but smile where others sob and screech.
The draggled flounces of the willows lash
My neck; I tread upon the bouncing rake,
Which bangs me sorely, but I hasten on,
With teeth firm-set as biting on a wire,
And feet and fingers clinched in bitter pain.

This, few would comprehend; but, if they did,
I should despise myself and merit scorn.
We all are riddles which we cannot guess ;
Each has his gimcracks and his thingumbobs,
And mine are night and nettles, mud and mist,
Since others hate them, cowardly avoid.
Things are mysterious when you make them so,
And the slow-pacing days are mighty queer ;
But Fate is at the bottom of it all,
And something somehow turns up in the end.

Zoïlus. That is an echo with a vengeance ! But the exaggeration of peculiarities is the best part of our fun ; there you had the advantage. And this proves what I have said, that the " classic " style is nearly impregnable. How *could* you exaggerate it ? You might as well undertake an architectural burlesque of the Parthenon. It is the Gothic, Byzantine, Moresque styles in literature which give the true material for travesty, just as they allow the greatest intellectual freedom.

The Ancient. We shall have to dub you "the Pugin of Poetry." You 've been taking a hint from Clough's *Bothie.*

The Gannet. Which Zoïlus does n't like, because of the hexameters, although there never were lighter and less encumbered lines. With all Clough's classicism, his is a thoroughly Saxon-Gothic mind. Where will you find a more remarkable combination of richness and subtlety, of scholarly finish and the frankest realism ? He is the only man who has ever made English phrase flow naturally in elegiac cadence. You, certainly, must remember, Ancient ?

"Where, upon Apennine slope, with the chestnut the oak-trees immingle,
  Where amid odorous copse bridle-paths wander and wind,
Where under mulberry branches the diligent rivulet sparkles,
  Or amid cotton and maize peasants their water-works ply,
Where, over fig-tree and orange in tier upon tier still repeated,
  Garden on garden upreared, balconies step to the sky, —
Ah, that I were, far away from the crowd and the streets of the city,
  Under the vine-trellis laid, O my beloved, with thee!"

ZOÏLUS. O, if you once begin to quote, I surrender.

THE ANCIENT. Let us all part on good terms; that is, each holding to his own opinion. [*Exeunt.*

NIGHT THE SIXTH.

(*Enter* Zoïlus, *last, the others being already assembled: he throws down a newspaper on the table.*)

Zoïlus. There! Read that notice of my last article in ———, and tell me whether such criticism is apt to encourage the development of an American literature!

The Gannet (*taking the paper*). I see where it is, by the dint of your thumb-nail; there are only half a dozen lines, in what I should call the sneering-oracular style; but, Zoïlus, you have yourself done a great deal of this thing. Now the poisoned chalice is commended to your own lips. It is singular how little sympathy we have for others, in such cases. When I am abused, somebody always sends the paper to me with lines drawn around the article, so that I shall not miss it; and all my friends are sure to ask, "Have you seen what So-and-so says?" When I am praised, nobody sends the paper, and my friends take it for granted that I have read the article. I don't complain of them: they are naturally silent when they agree, and aroused when they disagree, with the criticism.

The Ancient. This notice is not fair, of course; but it is only a part of the prevalent fashion of criticism.

One never can be sure, in such cases, whether the writer is really sincere in his judgment, or whether he has seized an opportunity to make a little literary capital for himself at the expense of the author. But I firmly believe in the ultimate triumph of *good work* over all these airs of superior knowledge and patronage and contemptuous depreciation. A friend of mine once devoted a great deal of time to a very careful and thorough article upon a poet who wrote in a dialect with which not ten men in this country are familiar. He afterwards showed me the critical notices it drew forth, and those which treated the subject with the coolest possible air of knowledge were written by men who knew nothing whatever about it.

GALAHAD. Then how is the ordinary reader ever to be enlightened?

THE ANCIENT. Most readers, I imagine, simply like, or dislike, what they read. Authors greatly exaggerate the effect of inadequate criticism. Why, do you know that critical genius is much rarer than poetical? You are not afraid of the crude poets, who publish in' newspaper corners, pushing you from your stools of song: why should you be annoyed by the critics who stand upon the same intellectual plane? Let me repeat to you what the greatest of critics, Lessing, said: " What is tolerable in my labors is owing solely to the critical faculty. I am, therefore, always ashamed or grieved whenever I hear anything said to the disadvantage of that faculty. It is said to crush genius, and I flattered myself that I had received in it something akin to genius." After Lessing, we can only accept Jeffrey with certain reservations, until we come to Sainte-Beuve. In this country, I call Lowell the first critic, though Whipple and Ripley have high and honorable places. A true critic must not only be a universal scholar, but as clear-conscienced as a saint and as tenderly impressible as a woman. After that he may be rigid as Minos.

Zoïlus. But you will certainly agree with me, that a critical literature of the kind you describe — intelligent, appreciative, sympathetic, and rigidly just — is much needed?

The Ancient. Never more than just now.

Zoïlus. What then, frankly, do you think of the tone of this paper, and the —— and the —— ?

The Ancient (*smiling*). They remind me so much of a little satirical poem of Uhland, "The Spring-Song of the Critic," that I am comforted and amused, when I might otherwise be most annoyed. There never was a more admirable picture of that fine, insidious egotism of the spurious critic, which makes him fear to praise, lest admiration should imply inferiority. I can't remember the original lines, or I would translate it for you; but I might try an American paraphrase.

Omnes. By all means! (The Ancient *writes*.)

Zoïlus. I feel as if I had had whiskey poured into an open wound. You made me smart savagely for a few minutes; but I am already getting comfortable.

The Gannet. There is no real comfort until you grow pachydermatous; I don't envy Galahad the seasoning that awaits him.

Galahad. I have part of my experience vicariously, in Zoïlus.

Zoïlus. The devil you have! wait, my boy, until you

publish your next poem: I'll return it to you, with interest!

THE ANCIENT. Uhland makes the critic walk out in the spring-time, and patronize Nature in his usual tone, the very tone of which Zoïlus complains. This is a rough imitation: —

H'm! Spring? 'T is popular, we've heard,
   And must be noticed, therefore;
Not that a flower, a brook, or bird
   Is what we greatly care for.

The trees are budding: immature!
   Yet them, no doubt, admire some:
One leaf comes like another, sure,
   And on the whole it's tiresome.

What kind of bird is this we hear?
   The song is vague and mystic;
Some notes, we grant, are smooth and clear,
   But not at all artistic.

We're not quite sure we wholly like
   Those ferns that wave and spread so:
'T is safe to doubt the things that strike
   The eye at once; we've said so.

An odor? H'm! it might be worse;
   There must be violets nigh us:
Quite passable! (For Shakespeare's verse,
   This time, will justify us.)

A native plant! We don't know what:
   Some, now, would call it pleasant,

But, really, we would rather not
    Commit ourselves, at present.

But further time we will not waste,
    Neglecting our position;
To scourge the stupid public taste
    Is our peculiar mission.

And if men saw us, and should deem
    (Those ignorant human brothers!)
That we the Spring *enjoyed*, we 'd seem
    No better than the others!

OMNES. Good! It reads like an original.

THE ANCIENT. It is one, properly: I have not translated any of Uhland's phrases. However, let us change the theme, for this is a dangerous hobby of mine, and we have other work before us. How many names are there still undrawn?

THE GANNET (*looking in the hat*). A dozen yet!

THE ANCIENT (*drawing*). James Russell Lowell,— I must gird up my loins.

THE GANNET. Bayard Taylor.

ZOÏLUS. Elizabeth Barrett Browning.

GALAHAD. George H. Boker.

THE GANNET. The supply will be exhausted in two or three nights more, and then all our fun must come to an end. There will be nothing left for us, but to travesty each other.

THE CHORUS. An excellent idea! Four times four, each doing each other and himself also, will give us sixteen imitations.

ZOÏLUS. No doubt you would enjoy it hugely. Turn to Lucretius for a picture of the delight of sitting on the safe shore and looking at the waves in a storm!

THE CHORUS. "The swelling and falling of the waves is the life of the sea."

ZOÏLUS. Go to, with your quotations! How easy it is to apply a high moral stimulus to somebody else's mind! Every poet, in his secret soul, admits his exquisite, quivering sensitiveness for the children of his brain. He may hide it from the sight of every one; but it is there, or he would not be a poet; and he is always most artlessly surprised at the betrayal of the same feeling in another. *I*, of course, should coolly bear any amount of travesty; but how would it be with the Ancient, the Gannet, and Galahad?

THE GANNET. Zoïlus, you're a humbug! Take your pencil and begin your work: see how the Ancient is reeling off his lines!

(*They write steadily for fifteen or twenty minutes; then all have finished except* THE ANCIENT.)

THE ANCIENT. Mine is no easy task, and I'm afraid I have laid it out on too extensive a plan.

OMNES. Go on: we will wait.

THE ANCIENT (*ten minutes later*). You will sympathize with me, Galahad, for you know how much I like Lowell's poetry. I have followed him from the start, when he seemed like a vigorous young oak, and like an oak he has grown slowly, strongly, and with ever-broadening branches. But one can sport, as well as pray, under your large trees. (*Reads.*)

THE SAGA OF AHAB DOOLITTLE.

Who hath not thought himself a poet? Who,
Feeling the stubbed pin-feathers pricking through
His greenish gosling-down, but straight misdeems
Himself anointed? They must run their course,
These later measles of the fledgling mind,
Pitting the adolescent rose with brown,
And after, leaving scars; and we must bear,
Who come of other stirp, no end of roil,
Slacken our strings, disorient ourselves,
And turn our ears to huge conchyliar valves
To hear the shell-hum that would fain be sea.

O guarding thorn of Life's dehiscent bud,
Exasperation! Did we clip thee close,
Disarm ourselves with non-resistant shears,
And leave our minds demassachusetted,
What fence 'gainst inroad of the spouting throng?
For Fame 's a bird that in her wayward sweep
Gossips to all; then, raven-like, comes home
Hoarse-voiced as autumn, and, as autumn leaves
Behind her, blown by all the postal winds,
Letters and manuscripts from unknown hands.
Thus came not Ahab's: his he brought himself,
One morn, so clear with impecunious gold,
I said: " Chaucer yet lives, and Calderon ! "
And, letting down the gangways of the mind
For shipment from the piers of common life,
O'er Learning's ballast meant some lighter freight
To stow, for export to Macarian Isles.
But it was not to be; a tauroid knock

Shook the ash-panels of my door with pain,
And to my vexed "Come in!" Ahab appeared.
Homespun, at least, — thereat I swiftly felt
Somewhat of comfort, — tall, knock-kneed, and gaunt :
Face windy-red, hands horny, large and loose,
That groped for mine, and finding, dropped at once
As half ashamed; and thereupon he grinned.
I waited, silent, till the silence grew
Oppressive; but he bore it like a man;
Then, as my face still queried, opened wide
The stiff portcullis of his rustic speech,
Whence issued words : "You 'd hardly kalkelate
That I 'm a poet, but I kind o' guess
I *be* one; so the people say, to hum."
Then from his cavernous armpit drew and gave
The singing leaves, not such as erst I knew,
But strange, disjointed, where the unmeasured feet
Staggered allwhither in pursuit of rhyme,
And could not find it : assonance instead,
Cases and verbs misplaced — remediable those —
Broad-shouldered coarseness, fondly meant for wit.
I turned the leaves; his small, gray, hungry eye
Stuck like a burr; agape with hope his mouth.
What could I say? the worn conventional phrase
We use on such occasions, — better wait,
Verse must have time; its seed, like timothy-grass,
Sown in the fall to sprout the following spring,
Is often winter-killed; none can decide;
A single rain-drop prints the eocene,
While crow-bars fail on lias: so with song :
The Doom is born in each thing's primitive stuff.

Perchance he understood not; yet I thrust

Some hypodermic hope within his flesh,
Unconsciously; erelong he came again.
Would I but see his latest? I *did* see;
Shuddered, and answered him in sterner wise.
I love to put the bars up, shutting out
My pasture from the thistle-cropping beasts
Or squealing hybrids, who have range enough
On our New England commons, — whom the Fiend,
Encouragement-of-Native-Talent, feeds
With windy provender, in Waverley,
And Flag, and Ledger, weakly manger-racks.

Months passed; the catbird on the elm-tree sang
What "Free from Ahab!" seemed, and I believed.
But, issuing forth one autumn morn, that shone
As Earth were made October twenty-seventh
(Some ancient Bible gives the date), he shot
Across my path as sped from Ensign's bow,
More grewsome, haggard-seeming than before.
Ere from his sinister armpit his right hand
Could pluck the sheets, I thundered forth, "Aroint!"
Not using the Anglo-Saxon shibboleth,
But exorcismal terms, unusual, fierce,
Such as would make a saint disintimate.
The witless terror in his face nigh stayed
My speech, but I was firm and passed him by.
Ah, not three weeks were sped, ere he again
Waylaid me in the meadows, with these words:
"I saw thet suthin' riled you, the last time;
Be you in sperrits now?" — and drew again —
But why go on? I met him yesterday,
The nineteenth time, — pale, sad, but patient still.

> When Hakon steered the dragons, there was place,
> Though but a thrall's, beside the eagle-helms,
> For him who rhymed instead of rougher work,
> For speech is thwarted deed: the Berserk fire
> But smoulders now in strange attempts at verse,
> While hammering sword-blows mend the halting rhyme,
> Give mood and tense unto the well-thewed arm,
> And turn these ignorant Ahabs into bards!

ZoÏlus. Faith! I think each of us imitates most amusingly the very authors whom he most admires. I might have made something fiercer, but it would n't have been more characteristic.

The Gannet. When you seem dissatisfied with Lowell's work, I can still see that you recognize his genius. I agree with you that he sometimes mistakes roughness for strength, and is sometimes consciously careless; but neither his faults nor his virtues are of the common order. I like him for the very quality out of which both grow, — his evident faith in the inspiration of the poet. In "The Cathedral" he says "second-thoughts are prose," which is always true of the prime conception; but he seems often to apply it to the details of verse. His sympathy with the Norse and Nibelungen elements in literature, and with the old English ballads, is natural and very strong. Perhaps it is not always smoothly fused with the other spirit which is born of his scholarship and taste and artistic feeling. I care less for that: to my mind, he is always grandly tonic and stimulating.

The Ancient. I think the objection which Zoilus makes comes simply from the fact that many of Lowell's poems are overweighted with ideas. Instead of pouring a thin, smooth stream, he tilts the bottle a little too much, and there is an impetuous, uneven crowding of thought. But I should rather say that he is like his own "Cathedral," large, Gothic, with many a flying buttress, pinnacles melting in the air, and now and then a grotesque gargoyle staring down upon you. There is a great range between Hosea Biglow and the Harvard Ode.

ZOÏLUS. I confess I don't like unmixed enthusiasm, and I'm frequently provoked to spy out the weak points of any author who gets much of it. How I should feel if it were bestowed on me, I can't tell; probably as complacent as the rest of you.

THE GANNET. O Zoïlus, when you know that *I*'m only considered "brilliant," and get the most superficial praise!

THE ANCIENT. Come, come! This is a sort of personality. Who's next?

GALAHAD. Zoïlus was ready first.

ZOÏLUS. Yes, and none too soon. Mrs. Barrett Browning was a tough subject for me, and I was glad to get her off my hands. Do you know that it is much more difficult to travesty a woman's poem than a man's? (*Reads.*)

GWENDOLINE.

'T was not the brown of chestnut boughs
   That shadowed her so finely;
It was the hair that swept her brows,
   And framed her face divinely;

Her tawny hair, her purple eyes,
  The spirit was ensphered in,
That took you with such swift surprise,
  Provided you had peered in.

Her velvet foot amid the moss
  And on the daisies patted,
As, querulous with sense of loss,
  It tore the herbage matted:
"And come he early, come he late,"
  She saith, "it will undo me;
The sharp fore-speeded shaft of fate
  Already quivers through me.

"When I beheld his red-roan steed,
  I knew what aim impelled it;
And that dim scarf of silver brede,
  I guessed for whom he held it:
I recked not, while he flaunted by,
  Of Love's relentless vi'lence,
Yet o'er me crashed the summer sky,
  In thunders of blue silence.

"His hoof-prints crumbled down the vale,
  But left behind their lava;
What should have been my woman's mail
  Grew jellied as guava:
I looked him proud, but 'neath my pride
  I felt a boneless tremor;
He was the Beer, I descried,
  And I was but the Seemer!

"Ah, how to be what then I seemed,
  And bid him seem that is so!

> We always tangle threads we dreamed,
>   And contravene our bliss so.
> I see the red-roan steed again!
>   He looks, as something sought he:
> Why, hoity-toity! — *he* is fain,
>   So *I*'ll be cold and haughty!"

THE ANCIENT. You have done about as well as could be expected; but I am not sure that I should have recognized it, without the red-roan steed and the thunders of blue silence. However, Mrs. Browning's force is always so truly feminine that one cannot easily analyze it. There is an underlying weakness — or, at least, a sense of reliance — when she is most vigorous, and you feel the beating of an excited pulse when she is most calmly classic. She often slips into questionable epithets and incongruous images, I grant you; but I can see the first form of her thought through them.

GALAHAD. Has any other woman reached an equal height in English poetry?

THE CHORUS. No!

THE GANNET. George Eliot?

ZOÏLUS. Now you bring the two squarely before my mind, I also say, No! I do not rightly know where to place George Eliot.

THE ANCIENT. Among the phenomena, — unsurpassed as a prose writer, and with every quality of the poet except the single one which is born and never acquired. It is amazing to see how admirable her verse is, and how near to high poetry, — as if only a sheet of plate-glass were between, — and yet it is *not* poetry. Her lines are like the dancing figures on a frieze, symmetry itself, but they do not move. When I read them, I am always on the very verge of recognizing her as a poet, always expecting the warm-blooded measures which sing their way into my own blood, and yet I never cross the invisible boundary.

The Gannet. Shall we go on? I have Bayard Taylor, who took possession of me readily enough. I know his earlier Oriental better than his later poems. He does n't seem to have any definite place yet as a poet.

Zoïlus. Then it comes of having too many irons in the fire.

Galahad. He may have made some mistakes; indeed, I think so, myself; but I find signs of a struggle towards some new form of development in his later poems, and mean to give him a little more opportunity. His rhetoric is at the same time his strength and his weakness, for it has often led him away from the true substance of poetry.

The Ancient. There you are right, Galahad. Nature and the sensuous delight of life for a while got the upper hand of him, and he wrote many things which aimed to be more, and were not. I think better of his later direction; but how far it will carry him depends on his industry and faith. Let us have the echo!

The Gannet. (*Reads.*)

HADRAMAUT.

The grand conglomerate hills of Araby
  That stand empanoplied in utmost thought,
With dazzling ramparts front the Indian sea,
  Down there in Hadramaut.

The sunshine smashes in the doors of morn
    And leaves them open; there the vibrant calm
Of life magniloquent pervades forlorn
        The giant fronds of palm.

The cockatoo upon the upas screams;
    The armadillo fluctuates o'er the hill;
And like a flag, incarnadined in dreams,
        All crimsonly I thrill!

There have iconoclasts no power to harm,
    So, folded grandly in translucent mist,
I let the light stream down my jasper arm,
        And o'er my opal fist.

An Adamite of old, primeval Earth,
    I see the Sphinx upon the porphyry shore,
Deprived of utterance ages ere her birth,
        As I am, — only more!

Who shall ensnare me with invested gold,
    Or paper symbols, backed like malachite?
Let gaunt reformers objurgate and scold,
        I gorge me with delight.

I do not yearn for what I covet most;
    I give the winds the passionate gifts I sought;
And slumber fiercely on the torrid coast,
        Down there in Hadramaut!

GALAHAD. That is extravagantly and absurdly like some of his poems. You seem to have had in your mind the very feature I mentioned, — his rhetoric. I doubt whether I shall succeed as well with Boker. He and

Bayard Taylor are both Pennsylvanians, of nearly the same age, yet they are not at all alike.

THE ANCIENT. I remember Boker's first volume. There was a flavor of the Elizabethan English about it, which was unusual at the time. Then came his tragedy of "Calaynos," one of the few successful modern plays formed on the old classic models; it ran for nearly a hundred nights in England. But you cannot imitate his best work, which is in this and the later plays; you must choose between his ballads and his sonnets.

GALAHAD. I have tried something half ballad and half song, in his style. (*Reads.*)

PHEBE THE FAIR.

I lie and I languish for Phebe the Fair,
      Ah, welladay!
The blue of her eyes, the brown of her hair,
The elbows that dance and the ankles that gleam,
As she bends at her washing-tub there by the stream,
Disdaining to see me, so what can I say
      But, ah, welladay!

I met her last night when the moon was at full,
      Alas and alack!
Bewitchingly hooded with mufflers of wool;
Her cloak of gray duffle she wore to a charm,
So boldly I offered the maiden my arm,
But she coolly responded, "You take the back track!"
      Alas and alack!

Though I 'm but a blacksmith and Hugo a lord,
      Sing hey, nonny nonny!

Though I 've but a hammer and he has a sword,
When he leans from his destrier Phebe to greet,
I could smash him to cinders before her white feet,
For lords have no business with maidens so bonny,
  Sing hey, nonny nonny!

I 've given up Margery, given up Maud,
  Ah, welladay, Phebe!
But the snow of your bosom by love is unthawed;
The hues of my life are all fading, I guess,
As the calico fades in the suds that you press:
You are scouring the heart of your languishing G. B.,
  Ah, welladay, Phebe!

THE GANNET. I remember those ballads, with a curious antique flavor about them; but I am best acquainted with Boker's sonnets. I don't think they have been appreciated as they deserve; but then, there are hardly twelve sonnets in the English language which can be called popular. Take one of Keats, three of Wordsworth, three of Milton, possibly Blanco White's one, and four or five of Shakespeare, and you have nearly all that are familiarly known. I 'll try my hand at an imitation of Boker's grave, sustained measure. (*Writes.*)

THE ANCIENT. No one of our authors is so isolated as he, and it is a double disadvantage. When Philadelphia ceased to be a literary centre, which happened very suddenly and unexpectedly, the tone of society there seemed to change. Instead of the open satisfaction of Boston in her brilliant circle of authors, or the passive indifference of our New York, there is almost a positive depreciation of home talent in Philadelphia. Boker is most disparaged in his native city, and most appreciated in New England. There is always less of petty envy where the range of culture is highest.

Zoïlus. No, there is not less, granting the culture to be higher; there is only more tact and policy in expressing it.

The Gannet. Listen to Boker's 999th sonnet, dictated through me! (*Reads.*)

> I charge not with degrees of excellence
> That fair revolt which rested on thy name,
> Nor burden with uncomprehended blame
> The speech, which still eludes my swooning sense,
> Though this poor rhyme at least were some defence
> Against thy chill suspicion: yet, if Fame
> Lift up and burnish what is now my shame,
> 'T would mitigate a passion so intense.
> This trampled verse awhile my heart relieves
> From stringent pain, that cleft me as I turned
> Away from beauty, graciously displayed;
> And still one dominant emotion cleaves
> The clouds, whereon thy passing lustre burned,
> And leaves behind it gulfs of blacker shade.

Galahad. How *could* you echo the tone and atmosphere of a sonnet, without adding one particle of sense?

The Gannet. Attribute it to my empty head, if you please. I really cannot explain how these imitations arise in my mind. In the "trance condition," you know, one is void of all active consciousness.

Zoïlus. If you go on indulging such an idea, you will end by becoming a professional medium.

The Gannet. Well, — at least I'll dictate to the world better verse than has ever yet come, in that way, from the unfortunate dead poets.

Galahad. Could you equal Demosthenes?

The Ancient. For the sake of Human Reason let us drop that subject! There are some aberrations which dishearten us, and it is best simply to turn our backs on them. For my part, I crave music. Zoïlus, give us Herrick's "Julia," before the stirrup-cup!

NIGHT THE SEVENTH.

THIS night the Gannet led the way to the more earnest conversation, by returning to a point touched by the Ancient at their fifth meeting. He said, "I should like to know wherein the period of fermentation, which precedes the appearance of an important era in literature, and the period of subsidence, or decadence, which follows it, differ from each other."

ZOÏLUS. H'm! that's rather a tough problem to be solved at a moment's warning. I should guess that the difference is something like that between the first and second childhood of an individual. In the first case, the faults are natural, heedless, graceful, and always suggestive of something to be developed; in the latter, they are helpless repetitions, which point only towards the past.

GALAHAD. Are you not taking the correspondence for granted? Is it exactly justified by the history of any great era in literature?

THE ANCIENT. Not entirely. But there is surely an irregular groping for new modes of thought and new forms of expression, in advance; and a struggle, after the masters of the age have gone, to keep up their pitch of achievement.

The Gannet. Very well; you are near enough in accord to consider my next question. In which period are we living at present? The Ancient says that we have had the heroes and the *epigonoi*, and that there will be many fallow years: I, on the contrary, feel very sure that we are approaching another great era; and the confusion of which he spoke the other night is an additional proof of it.

The Ancient. If you remember, I disclaimed any power of prediction.

The Gannet. So you did; but I insist that the reasons you gave are just as powerful against your conclusions, unless you can show us that the phenomena of our day are those which *invariably* characterize a period of decadence. I have been reflecting upon the subject with more earnestness than is usual to me. In our modern literature I do *not* find echoes of any other than the masters who are still living and producing, especially Browning, Longfellow, and Tennyson; the faint reflections of Poe seem to have ceased; and the chief characteristic of this day, so far as the younger authors are concerned, is a straining after novel effects, new costumes for old thoughts, if you please, but certainly something very different from a mere repetition of forms of style which already exist. That there is confusion, an absence of pure, clearly outlined ideals of art, I am willing to admit. I accept the premises, but challenge the inferences.

Galahad. I am only too ready to agree with you.

The Ancient. What I wish is, that we should try to comprehend the literary aspects of our time. If we can turn our modern habit of introversion away from our individual selves, and give it more of an objective character (though this sounds rather paradoxical), it will be a gain in every way. A period of decadence is not necessarily characterized by repetition; it may manifest itself in exactly such straining for effect as the Gannet admits. Poe, for instance, or Heine, or Browning, makes a new manner successful; what more natural, then, than that an inferior poet should say to himself, "The manner is everything; I will invent one for myself!" I find something too much of this prevalent, and it does not inspire me with hope.

Zoïlus. But the costume of the thought, as of the man, is really more important than the body it hides. And I insist that manner is more than symmetry, or even strength, as the French have been shrewd enough to discover. We are moving towards an equal brilliancy of style, only most of us are zigzagging on all sides of the true path. But we shall find it, and then, look out for a shining age of literature!

The Gannet (*to* The Ancient). You were speaking of the introversion which is such a characteristic of modern thought. Can a writer avoid it, without showing, in the very effort, that he possesses it?

The Ancient. I doubt it. Goethe tried the experiment, and did not fairly succeed. It seems to me that the character of an author is relative to the highest culture of his generation. I have never found that there was much development without self-study; for the true artist must know the exact measure of his qualities, in order to use them in his one true way. This is a law as applicable to Shakespeare as to you; but he may choose to conceal the process, and you may choose to betray it. For a poet to speculate upon his own nature, in his poems, is a modern fashion, which originated with Wordsworth. To us it seems an over-consciousness; yet it may seem the height of naïve candor, and therefore a delightful characteristic, to the critics of two centuries hence.

ZOÏLUS. Well, upon my word, Ancient, you are the most bewildering of guides! You talk of eternal laws, you refer to positive systems, but when we come to apply them, there is nothing permanent, nothing settled, only a labyrinth of perhapses and may-seems. What are we to do?

THE GANNET (*offering the hat*). To draw your name, and write.

ZOÏLUS (*drawing*). Julia Ward Howe: and I feel no mission within me! I shall miserably fail.

THE GANNET. Jean Ingelow: I need no mission.

GALAHAD. The saints help me! Walt Whitman.

THE ANCIENT. Buchanan Read: *I* must call on the Pope, to judge from the last poem of his which I have read. There are but one or two more slips in the hat: whom have we? Piatt, Bret Harte, Joaquin Miller! Galahad, I suggest that you return our yawping cosmos, and take Piatt in his stead; then let us add John Hay, and we shall have all the latest names together for our next and final night of diversions.

THE GANNET. I second your proposal. It will separate the last and most curious phenomena in poetry from those which preceded them. Perhaps we may be able to guess what they portend.

GALAHAD (*changing the name*). I am so grateful for the permission, that I will write two; adding to the imitation of Piatt that of the author of "A Woman's Poems," in whose poetical fortunes, I imagine, he feels more interest than even in his own. I am attracted by her poems as the Gannet is attracted by Mrs. Stoddard's, though the two are wholly unlike. In "The Woman" I also see indications of a struggle between thought and language, a reluctance to catch the flying Psyche by the wings, and hold her until every wavering outline is clear. Women-poets generally stand in too much awe of their own conceptions.

ZOÏLUS (*solemnly*). I am possessed! *Procul, O procul*, — or at least be silent. (*Writes.*)

(*All write steadily, and finish their tasks nearly at the same time.*)

THE CHORUS. You came up so nearly neck and neck, that only we who timed you can decide. The Gannet first.

THE GANNET. Then hearken to Jean Ingelow. (*Reads.*)

THE SHRIMP-GATHERERS.

Scarlet spaces of sand and ocean,
    Gulls that circle and winds that blow;
Baskets and boats and men in motion,
    Sailing and scattering to and fro.

Girls are waiting, their wimples adorning
    With crimson sprinkles the broad gray flood;

And down the beach the blush of the morning
  Shines reflected from moisture and mud.

Broad from the yard the sail hangs limpy;
  Lightly the steersman whistles a lay;
Pull with a will, for the nets are shrimpy,
  Pull with a whistle, our hearts are gay!

Tuppence a quart; there are more than fifty!
  Coffee is certain, and beer galore:
Coats are corduroy, minds are thrifty,
  Won't we go it on sea and shore!

See, behind, how the hills are freckled
  With low white huts, where the lasses bide!
See, before, how the sea is speckled
  With sloops and schooners that wait the tide!

Yarmouth fishers may rail and roister,
  Tyne-side boys may shout, "Give way!"
Let them dredge for the lobster and oyster,
  Pink and sweet are our shrimps to-day!

Shrimps and the delicate periwinkle,
  Such are the sea-fruits lasses love:
Ho! to your nets till the blue stars twinkle,
  And the shutterless cottages gleam above!

THE CHORUS. A very courteous echo. The Ancient was next.

THE ANCIENT. I think if Buchanan Read had confined himself to those short, sweet, graceful lyrics by which he first became known, he would have attained a better success. It is singular, by the by, that his art does not color his poetry, as in Rossetti's case; no one could guess that he is also a painter. But I remember that Washington Allston is a similar instance. Read's best poems are those which have a pastoral character, and I have turned to them for his characteristic manner. (*Reads.*)

A SYLVAN SCENE.

The moon, a reaper of the ripened stars,
    Held out her silver sickle in the west;
I leaned against the shadowy pasture-bars,
    A hermit, with a burden in my breast.

The lilies leaned beside me as I stood;
    The lilied heifers gleamed beneath the shed;
And spirits from the high ancestral wood
    Cast their articulate benisons on my head.

The twilight oriole sang her valentine
    From pendulous nests above the stable-sill,
And like a beggar, asking alms and wine,
    Came the importunate murmur of the mill.

Love threw his flying shuttle through my woof,
    And made the web a pattern I abhorred;
Wherefore alone I sang, and far aloof,
    My melting melodies, mightier than the sword.

The white-sleeved mowers, coming slowly home,
    With scythes like rainbows on their shoulders hung,
Sniffed not, in passing me, the scent of Rome,
    Nor heard the music trickling from my tongue.

The milkmaid, following, delayed her step,
  Still singing as she left the stable-yard:
'T was "Sheridan's Ride" she sang: I turned and wep',
  For woman's homage soothes the suffering bard!

GALAHAD. Why did n't you take Read's "Drifting"?

THE ANCIENT. It is a beautiful poem, but would betray itself in any imitation. My object was to catch his especial poetic dialect.

THE CHORUS. Now, Zoïlus.

ZOÏLUS. I have followed exactly the Ancient's plan, but with the disadvantage of not having read Mrs. Howe's "Passion Flowers" lately; so I was forced to take whatever features were accessible, from her prose as well as verse. (*Reads.*)

THE COMING RACE.

When with crisped fingers I have tried to part
  The petals which compose
The azure flower of high æsthetic art,
  More firmly did they close.

Yet woman is not undeveloped man, —
  So singeth Tennyson:
Desire, that ever Duty's feet outran,
  Begins, but sees not done.

Our life is full of passionate dismay
  At larger schemes grown small;
That which thou doest, do this very day,
  Then art thou known of all.

The thing that was ungerms the thing to be;
    Before reflects Behind;
So blends our moral trigonometry
    With spheroids of the mind.

Time shall transfigure many a paradox,
    Now crushed with hoofs of scorn,
When in the beauty of the hollyhocks
    The Coming Man is born.

His hand the new Evangels then shall hold,
    That make earth epicene,
And on his shoulder, coiffed with chrismal gold,
    The Coming Woman lean!

THE GANNET. O, she should not lean on his shoulder! That is a dependent attitude.

ZOÏLUS. I know; but there is the exigency of an immediate rhyme, and "epicene" is a word which I could not sacrifice.

THE ANCIENT. You have hit upon one of the vices of our literary class, — the superficial refinement which vents itself on words and phrases. I have seen expressions of both love and grief which were too elegant for passion. The strong thought always finds the best speech, but as its total form: it does not pause to prink itself by the way, or to study its face in a glass. I beg pardon, Zoïlus; I am not speaking of, but *from*, you.

ZOÏLUS. As the sinner furnishes more texts than the saint.

THE CHORUS. Let us not keep Galahad waiting.

GALAHAD. I promised two, but have only finished the first. The Gannet must keep me company; for we were nigh forgetting William Winter, and he must be entertained before our board is cleared for the last comers. I dare say we shall remember others; indeed, I can think of several who ought to please the Ancient, for they simply give us their ideas without any manner at all.

The Ancient. Sarcasm from Galahad is sarcasm indeed! I am assailed on all sides, to-night. But let us have Piatt; we have all looked through his "Western Windows."

Galahad. (*Reads.*)

THE OLD FENCE-RAIL.

It lies and rots by the roadside,
    Among the withering weeds;
The blackberry-vines run o'er it,
    And the thistles drop their seeds.

Below, the Miami murmurs;
    He flows as he always flowed;
And the people, eastward and westward,
    Travel the National Road.

At times a maiden's glances
    Gild it with tints of dawn,
But the school-boy snorts with his nostrils,
    Kicks it, and hastens on.

Above it the pioneer's chimney,
    Lonely and rickety, leans;
Beside it the pioneer's garden
    Is a wildering growth of greens.

It was split by the stalwart settler,
    One of the ancient race,
And the hands of his tow-haired children
    Lifted it into its place.

Years after the gawky lover
    Sat on it, dangling his heels,
While his girl forgot her milking,
    And the pen, with its hungry squeals.

Ah, the rail has its own romances,
    The scenes and changes of years:
I pause whenever I see it,
    And drop on it several tears.

Zoïlus. Don't you all feel, with me, that our imitations become more and more difficult as we take the younger authors who give us sentiment, fancy, pure metres, — in short, very agreeable and meritorious work, — but who neither conquer us by their daring nor provoke us by offending our tastes?

The Ancient. We foresaw this, the first evening, you will remember. There are many excellent poets, who cannot be amusingly travestied, — Collins, or Goldsmith, for example. I was just deliberating whether to suggest the names of two women who have written very good poems, Lucy Larcom and she who calls herself "H. H." The former has rhetoric and rhythm, and uses both quite independently; her "Hannah Binding Shoes" struck an original vein, which I wish she had gone on quarrying. But her finest poem, "The Rose Enthroned," could only be appreciated by about one per cent of her readers. "H. H." shows delicacy and purity of sentiment, yet her verse is not precisely *song*. Her ear fails to catch the rarer music which lurks behind metrical correctness. I don't well see how either could be imitated; so we will leave the Gannet and Galahad to their second task.

The Gannet (*looking up*). What you have been saying also applies to my present model. Just the best poems in his "Witness" are so simple, so sweetly and smoothly finished, so marked by pure taste and delicate fancy, that a good travesty would have the air of a serious imitation.

Zoïlus (*to the* Ancient). However we may disagree, I heartily join you in relishing a marked individuality in poetry.

The Ancient. When it is honest, when it frankly expresses the individual nature, not too much restricted by the conventionalisms of the day, nor yielding too indolently to the influences of other minds. It is a notable characteristic of nearly all our younger poets, that they wander, as if at random, over such a wide field, before selecting their separate paths. One cause of this, I should guess, is the seduction exercised by that refinement in form, that richness and variety of metrical effect, which marks our modern poetry. Twenty years ago, our only criticism almost ignored the idea in a poem; it concerned itself with words, lines, or stanzas, italicizing every agreeable little touch of fancy, as a guide to the reader. Leigh Hunt made this fashion popular; Poe imitated him; and our young authors were taught to believe in detached beauties of expression, instead of pure and symmetrical conceptions. Take the earlier poems of Stoddard, Read,

Aldrich, Bayard Taylor, and others, and you cannot fail to see how they were led astray.

Zoïlus. Then, I suppose, their genuine poetical quality is tested by the extent to which they have emancipated themselves from those early influences, and discovered their proper individualities?

The Ancient. Most certainly; and if you had grown up with the generation, as I have (being very little older), you would see, as I do now, how each is struggling out of the general wilderness. Boker had not far to go; he grew up under the broad wings of the old English dramatists. Stoddard first struck his highest performance in "The Fisher and Charon," and Stedman in his "Alectryon," though both are still best known by their lighter lyrics. Aldrich seems now to be aware of his native grace and delicacy of fancy, and Howells of the sportive, lightsome element, which the *Weltschmerz* of youth for a time suppressed. In his "Pastorals," Bayard Taylor seems inclined to seek for the substance of poetry, rather than the flash and glitter of its rhetorical drapery. Piatt is turning more and more to that which lies nearest him: in short, without pretending to decide how far each is successful, I think that each, now, is attending seriously to his own special work.

Zoïlus. How much longer do you give them, to reach their highest planes of performance?

The Ancient. All their lives; and I refer you to Bryant, Emerson, Longfellow, and Whittier, as instances of continuous development. If our American atmosphere, as you said the other night, retards the growth of literary men, you cannot deny that it wonderfully prolongs the period of their growth.

THE GANNET. Here have Galahad and myself been waiting with our manuscripts, knowing that you two can never agree, but hoping that each might exhaust the other.

ZOÏLUS. This from you, for whom there is neither time, space, nor place, when you get fairly started! But who are you now?

THE GANNET. William Winter, at your service. (*Reads.*)

LOVE'S DIET.

There be who crave the flavors rich
    Of boneless turkey and of beef;
There be who seek the relish which
    To palsied palates brings relief:
But I, in love's most patient hush,
Partake with thee of simple mush.

The pheasant seems so bright of wing,
    Because 't is wedded with expense;
The rarer Strasburg pasties bring
    But fleet enjoyment to the sense;
Yet common things, that seem too nigh,
Both purse and heart may satisfy.

'T is sweet to browse on dishes rare,
    When those who give them can afford:
Sweeter this unpretending fare,
    When thou art seated at the board,
With spoony fingers to unfold
The yielding mush's mass of gold.

> Thou pour'st the milk that whiter seems
>   Than is the orbit of thy brow,
> And I indulge with lamb-like dreams,
>   And many a white and harmless vow;
> I only wish that there could be
> One bowl, not two, for thee and me.

ZOÏLUS. I was not expecting even so much success.

THE GANNET. Galahad was generous, to give me the lighter task. It would have quite bewildered me to imitate "A Woman's Poems," because their chief characteristic is a psychological one. If we had taken that wonderful volume of the songstresses of the "South-Land," now —

ZOÏLUS. That reminds me of a graceful Southern singer, who is like a bard alone in the desert, — Paul H. Hayne. Talk of *our* lack of sympathy and encouragement, here, in New York! What mate has he, for hundreds of miles around him? Why, there is not even the challenge of a rival lance; he must ride around the lonely lists, with neither antagonist to prove his mettle, nor queen to crown him for success.

THE ANCIENT. An author *must* have an audience, however thin. We are told that Poetry is its own exceeding great reward: very well: but what if you sing your song into the air and never find it again in the heart of a friend? Genius without sympathetic recognition is like a kindled fire without flue or draught; it smoulders miserably away instead of leaping, sparkling, and giving cheer. I have seen some parts of the country where a man of sensitive, poetical nature would surely die, if he could not escape. We ought to be very tender towards all honest efforts in literature.

Galahad. The "Woman" whom I have imitated needs only the encounter of kind, yet positive minds, to give her dreams what they still lack, — a distinct reality. I have purposely tried to exaggerate her principal fault, for it was the only thing I could do. (*Reads.*)

THE PLASTER CAST.

The white thought sleeps in it enshrined,
    Though mean and cheap the substance seems,
As sleep conceptions in the mind,
    Hardened, and unreleased by dreams.

A parrot only! yet the child
    Stares with untutored, dim surprise,
And fain would know what secret mild
    Is ambushed in those moveless eyes.

His cherry from the painted beak
    Falls, when his gentle hand would give,
So early some return we seek
    From that which only seems to live.

Ah, let us even these symbols guard,
    Nor shatter them with curious touch;
For, should we break ideals hard,
    The fragments would not move us much.

Zoïlus. You have fairly bewildered me, Galahad. I thought there was an actual idea in the verses, but it slips from my hand like an eel.

The Ancient. It would better answer for the travesty of a school which has a limited popularity at present, but to which "A Woman" does not belong.

Galahad. What school? I know of none such.

The Ancient. The most active members would no doubt be much astonished if I were to tell them of it; but it is a kind of school, nevertheless. I think it must have originated as long ago as the days of *The Dial*, and has not yet wholly gone out of fashion with a rather large class of readers. You will find plenty of specimens in newspapers of a mixed religious and literary character, and now and then in the magazines.

The Chorus. Give us its peculiarities.

The Ancient. First, great gravity, if not solemnity of tone; a rhythm, sometimes weak, sometimes hard, but usually halting; obscurity and incoherence of thought, and a perpetual reference to abstract morality.

Zoïlus. Don't describe, but imitate.

The Ancient. I could give you a stanza, by way of illustration. Furnish me with a subject,— anything you please. (Zoïlus *writes*.) *The Fifth Wheel!* that will answer; for the poets of this school always begin far away from their themes. The first stanza might run thus:—

> From sunshine and from moral truth
>   Let Life be woven athwart thy breast!
> The rapid cycles of thy youth
>   But fetter Duty's solemn quest.

Omnes. Go on!

The Ancient. Now I may get a little nearer to

the subject, though I don't clearly see how. (*After a pause.*)

> Vibration gives but faint assent
>   To that which in thee seems complete,
> But time evolves the Incident
>   Behind the dust-driven chariot's feet.
>
> Be well provided! Overplus
>   Is Life's stern law, none can evade;
> Thou to the goal shalt hasten thus,
>   When selfish natures' wheels are stayed.

ZOÏLUS. Great Jove! to think that I never discovered the undying Laura Matilda in this prim disguise! It is the languishing creature grown older, with a high-necked dress, a linen collar, and all her curls brushed smooth! Ancient, you have purged mine eyes from visual film; this boon wipes out all remembrance of our strife.

OMNES. Enough for to-night! [*Exeunt.*

NIGHT THE EIGHTH.

(All the members promptly on hand.)

HE CHORUS. How much does any author distinctly know of himself, or the quality of his works?

ZOÏLUS. Not much.

GALAHAD. Everything!

THE GANNET. Only what makes a hit, and what does n't.

THE ANCIENT. It depends on who and what the author is: you will find both extremes represented.

THE CHORUS. Yourselves, for instance!

ZOÏLUS. To be frank, I think I have more merit than luck. But when I come to contrast the degrees of popularity with the character of the performance, I am puzzled.

GALAHAD. Popularity has nothing to do with it. I know that some of my qualities are genuine, while other necessary ones are weakly represented. Our talk, the last night, satisfied me that I have not yet found the one best direction; but, on the other hand, one dare not force one's own development, and I think I see whither I am tending.

The Gannet. Do you want to see where you stand now, or very nearly the spot?

Galahad. Show me if you can?

(The Gannet *takes a sheet of paper and writes.*)

Zoïlus (*to* The Ancient). Do you think that a poet is generally a correct judge of his own works?

The Ancient. Please, don't repeat that dismal platitude! A genuine poet is *always* the best judge of his own works, simply because he has an ideal standard by which he measures whatever he does. He may not be able to guess what will be most popular; he may attach an exorbitant value to that which is born of some occult individual mood, in which few others can ever share; but in regard to the quality of the calm, ripened product of his brain he cannot be mistaken! To admit that he can be, substitutes chance for law in the poetic art, and brings us down to the vulgar idea of a wayward and accidental inspiration, instead of conscious growth followed by conscious achievement.

Zoïlus. You astonish me.

The Ancient. Then be glad; it is a sign that you are not poetically *blasé*.

Galahad. Never! One can never be that.

The Gannet. Wait till you hear how your theorbo sounds in my ears. What I have attempted is a serious, not a comical, echo of your style.

Omnes. Give it to us!

The Gannet. Keep Galahad's hands off me till I have finished. (*Reads.*)

THE TWO LIVES.

Down in the dell I wandered,
    The loneliest of our dells,
Where grow the lowland lilies,
    Dropping their foam-white bells,
And the brook among the grasses
    Toys with its sand and shells.

Fair were the meads and thickets,
    And sumptuous grew the trees,
And the folding hills of harvest
    Were lulled with the fanning breeze,
But I heard, beyond the valley,
    The roar of the plunging seas.

The birds and the vernal grasses,
    They wooed me sweetly and long,
But the magic of ocean called me,
    Murmuring vast and strong;
Here was the flute-like cadence,
    There was the world-wide song!

"Lie in the wood's embraces,
    Sleep in the dell's repose!"
"Float on the limitless azure,
    Flecked with its foamy snows!"
Such were the changing voices,
    Heard at the twilight's close.

Free with the winds and waters,
    Nestled in shade and dew;

>   Bliss in the soft green shelter,
>   Fame on the boundless blue;
>   Which shall I yield forever?
>   Which forever pursue?

OMNES (*clapping their hands*). Galahad! Galahad!

GALAHAD (*with a melancholy air*). It is worse than the most savage criticism. There is just enough of my own sentiment and poetical manner in it, to show me how monstrously blind I have been in not perceiving that scores of clever fellows may write the same things, if they should choose. I ought to relapse into the corner of a country newspaper.

THE ANCIENT. Take heart, my dear boy! We all begin with sentiment and melodious rhythm, — or what seems to us to be such. We all discover the same old metaphors over again, and they are as new to us as if they had never been used before. Very few young poets have the slightest presentiment of their coming development. They have the keenest delight, the profoundest satisfaction, with their crudest works. With knowledge comes the sense of imperfection, which increases as they rise in performance. Remember that the Gannet is five or six years older than you, and can now write in cold blood what only comes from the summer heat of your mind.

GALAHAD. I understand you, and don't mean to be discouraged. But Zoïlus is fully avenged now.

ZOÏLUS. I'll prove it by my notice of your next poem in the ——. Let us turn to our remaining models. Whatever may be thought of them at home, they have all made a very positive impression in England; how do you account for it, Ancient?

The Ancient. I can only guess at an explanation, apart from the merits which three of them certainly possess. While the average literary culture in England was perhaps never so high as now, the prevalent style of writing was never so conventional. The sensational school, which has been so popular here as well as there, is beginning to fatigue the majority of readers, yet it still spoils their enjoyment of simple, honest work; so, every new appearance in literature, which is racy, which carries the flavor of a fresh soil with it, unconventional yet seemingly natural, neither suggesting the superficial refinement of which they are surfeited nor the nobler refinement which they have forgotten how to relish, — all such appearances, I suspect, furnish just the change they crave.

The Gannet. But the changes of popular taste in the two countries are very similar. This is evident in the cases of Bret Harte and Hay; but Walt Whitman seems to have a large circle of enthusiastic admirers in England, and only some half-dozen disciples among us. Do you suppose that the passages of his "Leaves of Grass," which are prose catalogues to us, or the phrases which are our slang, have a kind of poetical charm there, because they are not understood?

Zoïlus. As Tartar or Mongolian "Leaves of Grass" might have to us? Very likely. There are splendid lines and brief passages in Walt Whitman: there is a modern, half-Bowery-boy, half-Emersonian apprehension of the old Greek idea of physical life, which many take to be wholly new on account of the singular form in which it is presented. I will even admit that the elements of a fine poet exist in him, in a state of chaos. It is curious that while he proclaims his human sympathies to be without bounds, his intellectual sympathies should be so narrow. There never was a man at once so arrogant, and so tender towards his fellow-men.

The Ancient. You have very correctly described him. The same art which he despises would have increased his power and influence. He forgets that the poet must not only have somewhat to say, but must strenuously acquire the power of saying it most purely and completely. A truer sense of art would have prevented that fault which has been called immorality, but is only a coarse, offensive frankness.

The Gannet. Let us divide our labors. There is only one name apiece: how shall we apportion them?

Zoïlus. Take Joaquin Miller, and give Walt Whitman to the Ancient. Choose of these two, Galahad!

Galahad (*opening the paper*). Bret Harte.

Zoïlus. Then Hay remains to me.

(*They all write steadily for half an hour.*)

The Gannet. Our last is our most difficult task; for we have to give the local flavor of the poetry, as well as its peculiar form and tone.

Zoïlus. I should like to know how much of that local flavor is genuine. I am suspicious of Bret Harte's California dialect: some features of it are evidently English, and very suggestive of Dickens. Hay's is nearer the real thing. Miller's scenery and accessories also inspire me with doubt. Now, much of the value of this *genre* poetry (as I should call it) depends upon its fidelity to nature.

Sham slang and sham barbarism are worse than sham refinement and luxury.

THE ANCIENT. Harte's use of "which" as an expletive is certainly an English peculiarity, which he may have heard it in some individual miner, but which it is not a feature of California slang. So, when Miggles says "O, if you please, I'm Miggles," it is an English girl who speaks. Aside from a few little details of this kind, Harte's sketches and poems are truly and admirably colored. He deserves his success, for he has separated himself by a broad gulf from all the literary buffoonery of this day, which is sometimes grotesque and always inane. But he is *picturesque,* and the coarsest humor of his characters rests on a pure human pathos.

GALAHAD. Somehow, the use of a vulgar dialect in poetry is always unpleasant to me; it is like a grinning mask over a beautiful face. And yet, how charming is "'Zekel's Courtship"!

THE ANCIENT. Lowell has done all that is possible with the New England dialect. He has now and then steeped it in an odor of poetry which it never before exhaled and perhaps never may again. Compare it, for instance, with the Scotch of Burns, where every elision makes the word sweeter on the tongue, and where the words which are its special property are nearly always musical. The New England changes are generally on the side of roughness and clumsiness. *With* becomes an ugly *'th,* instead of the soft Scotch *wi'*; *have* hardens into *hev,* instead of flowing into *hae;* and *got* coarsens into *gut,* instead of the quaint sharpness of *gat.* It is the very opposite of the mellow broadness of the Scotch; it sacrifices the vowels and aggravates the consonants; its raciest qualities hint of prevarication and noncommital, and its sentiment is grotesque even when it is frank and touching. Yet Lowell's genius sometimes so completely transfigures this harsh material, that one's ear forgets it and hears only the finer music of his thought.

Zoïlus. Shall we read? I suggest that we take the authors, to-night, in the order of their appearance. Walt Whitman leads.

The Ancient. (*Reads.*)

CAMERADOS.

Everywhere, everywhere, following me;
Taking me by the buttonhole, pulling off my boots, hustling me with the elbows;
Sitting down with me to clams and the chowder-kettle;
Plunging naked at my side into the sleek, irascible surges;
Soothing me with the strain that I neither permit nor prohibit;
Flocking this way and that, reverent, eager, orotund, irrepressible;
Denser than sycamore leaves when the north-winds are scouring Paumanok;
What can I do to restrain them? Nothing, verily nothing.
Everywhere, everywhere, crying aloud for me;
Crying, I hear; and I satisfy them out of my nature;
And he that comes at the end of the feast shall find something over.
Whatever they want I give; though it be something else, they shall have it.
Drunkard, leper, Tammanyite, small-pox and cholera patient, shoddy, and codfish millionnaire,

And the beautiful young men, and the beautiful young women,
    all the same,
Crowding, hundreds of thousands, cosmical multitudes,
Buss me and hang on my hips and lean up to my shoulders,
Everywhere listening to my yawp and glad whenever they
    hear it;
Everywhere saying, say it, Walt, we believe it:
Everywhere, everywhere.

ZoÏlus. By Jove, Ancient! you could soon develop into a Kosmos.

The Ancient. It would not be difficult, so far as the form is concerned. The immortal Tupper, in his rivalry with Solomon, substituted semi-rhythmical prose lines for verse; but Walt, being thoroughly in earnest, often makes his lines wholly rhythmical. I confess I enjoy his decameters and hecatameters.

The Chorus. Bret Harte was the next appearance, after a very long interval. You will have to do your best, Galahad.

Galahad. A superficial imitation is easy enough, but I shall certainly fail to reproduce his subtile wit and pathos. (*Reads.*)

TRUTHFUL JAMES'S SONG OF THE SHIRT.

    Which his name it was Sam;
      He had sluiced for a while
    Up at Murderer's Dam,
      Till he got a good pile,
    And the heft of each dollar,
      Two thousand or more,

He'd put in the Chollar,
    For he seed it was ore
That runs thick up and down, without ceilin' or floor.

And, says he, it's a game
    That's got but one stake;
If I put up that same,
    It'll bust me or make.
At fifty the foot
    I've entered my pile,
And the whole derned cahoot
    I'll let soak for a while,
And jest loaf around here, — say, Jim, will you smile?

Tom Fakes was the chum,
    Down in Frisco, of Sam;
And one mornin' there come
    This here telegram:
"You can sell for five hundred,
    Come down by the train!"
Sam By-Joed and By-Thundered, —
    'T was whistlin' quite plain,
And down to Dutch Flat rushed with might and with main.

He had no time to sarch,
    But he grabbed up a shirt
That showed bilin' and starch,
    And a coat with less dirt.
He jumped on the step
    As the train shoved away,
And likewise was swep',
    All galliant and gay,
Round the edge of the mountin and down to'rds the Bay.

Seven minutes, to pass
    Through the hole by the Flat!

Says he, I'm an ass
  If I can't shift in that!
But the train behind time,
  Only *three* was enough, —
It came pat as a rhyme —
  He was stripped to the buff
When they jumped from the tunnel to daylight! 'T was rough.

  What else? Here's to you!
    Which he sold of his feet
  At five hundred, 't is true,
    And the same I repeat:
  But acquaintances, friends,
    They likes to divert,
  And the tale never ends
    Of Sam and his shirt,
And to stop it from goin' he'd give all his dirt!

ZOÏLUS. You were right to take a merely comical incident. You could n't possibly have echoed the strong feeling which underlies the surface slang of such a poem as "Jim," which I consider Harte's masterpiece in his special vein.

GALAHAD. He never could have written that if he had been only a humorist. His later work shows that he is a genuine poet.

THE ANCIENT. Yes, that special vein is like many in the Nevada mines, rich on the surface, narrowing as it goes down, pinched off by the primitive strata, opening again unexpectedly into a pocket, but never to be fully depended upon. Harte's instincts are too true not to see this: I believe he will do still better, and therefore probably less popular work.

The Gannet. Now, Zoïlus, give us Hay, and let *me* close with a war-whoop!

Zoïlus. I'm not quite sure of my Pike dialect, but I fancy the tone is rough enough to satisfy you. (*Reads.*)

BIG BILL.

There's them that eats till they're bustin',
    And them that drinks till they're blind,
And them that's snufflin' and spooney,
    But the best of all, to my mind,
(And I've been around in my time, boys,
    And cavorted with any you like,)
Was Big Bill, that lived in the slashes,
    We called him Big Bill o' Pike.

If he put his hand to his bowie
    Or scratched the scruff of his neck,
You could only tell by waitin'
    To see if you bled a peck:
And the way he fired, 't was lovely!
    Nobody knowed which was dead,
Till Big Bill grinned, and the stiff 'un
    Tumbled over onto his head!

At school he killed his master;
    Courtin', he killed seven more:
And the hearse was always a-waitin'
    A little ways from his door.
There was n't much growth in the county,
    As the census returns will show,
But we had Big Bill we was proud of,
    And that was enough to grow.

> And now Big Bill is an angel, —
>   Damn me, it makes me cry!
> Jist when he was rampin' the roughest,
>   The poor fellow had to die.
> A thievin' and sneakin' Yankee
>   Got the start on our blessed Bill,
> And there's no one to do our killin'
>   And nobody left to kill!

ZOÏLUS. Hay's realism, in those ballads, is of the grimmest kind. It is like the old Dance of Death, in a new form. I have been greatly amused by the actual fury which his "Little Breeches" and "Jim Bludso" have aroused in some sectarian quarters. To read the attacks, one would suppose that Christianity was threatened by the declaration that angels may interpose to save children, or that a man, ignorant or regardless of ordinary morality, may redeem his soul by the noblest sacrifice. Really, it seems to me, that to diminish the range of individual damnation renders many good people unhappy.

THE ANCIENT. Hay has made his name known in the most legitimate way, — by representing phenomena of common Western life which he has observed. He might have faintly echoed Shelley or Tennyson for a decade, and accomplished nothing. Those ballads are not, strictly speaking, poetry; but it is impossible that they should not give him a tendency to base his better poems on the realities of our American life.

THE CHORUS. Let us hear the Gannet's war-whoop!

THE GANNET. There is nothing easier than to exaggerate exaggeration. (*Reads.*)

THE FATE OF THE FRONTIERSMAN.

That whiskey-jug! For, dry or wet,
My tale will need its help, you bet!

We made for the desert, she and I,
Though life was loathsome, and love a lie,
And she gazed on me with her glorious eye,
But all the same, — I let her die!
For why? — there was barely water for one
In the small canteen, and of provender, none!
A splendid snake, with an emerald scale,
Slid before us along the trail,
With a famished parrot pecking its head;
And, seizing a huge and dark brown rock
In her dark brown hands, as you crush a crock,
With the dark brown rock she crushed it dead.
But ere her teeth in its flesh could meet,
I laid her as dead as the snake at my feet,
And grabbed the snake for myself to eat.

The plain stretched wide, from side to side,
As bare and blistered and cracked and dried
As a moccasin sole of buffalo hide,
And my throat grew hot, as I walked the trail,
My blood in a sizzle, my muscles dry,
A crimson glare in my glorious eye,
And I felt my sinews wither and fail,
Like one who has lavished, for fifty nights,
His pile in a hell of gambling delights,
And is kicked at dawn from bottle and bed,
And sent to the gulches without a red.

There was no penguin to pick or pluck,
No armadillo's throat to be stuck,
Not even a bilberry's ball of blue
To slush my tongue with its indigo dew,
And the dry brown palm-trees rattled and roared
Like the swish and swizzle of Walker's sword.
I was nigh rubbed out; when, far away,
A shanty baked in the furnace of day,
And I petered on, for an hour or more,
Till I dropped, like a mangy hound, at the door.

No soul to be seen; but a basin stood
On the bench, with a mess of dubious food,
Stringy and doughy and lumpy and thick,
As the clay ere flame has turned it to brick.
I gobbled it up with a furious fire,
A prairie squall of hungry desire,
And strength came back; when, lo! a scream
Closed my stomach and burst my dream.
She stood before me, as lithe and tall
As a musqueet-bush on the Pimos wall,
Fierce as the Zuñi panther's leap,
Fair as the slim Apache sheep.
A lariat draped her broad brown hips,
As she stood and glared with parted lips,
While piercing stitches and maddening shoots
Ran through my body, from brain to boots.
I would have clasped her, but, ere I could,
She flung back her hair's tempestuous hood,
And screamed, in a voice like a tiger-cat's:
"You've gone and ett up my pizen for rats!"
My blood grew limp and my hair grew hard
As the steely tail of the desert pard:

I sank at her feet, convulsed and pale,
And kissed in anguish her brown toe-nail.
You may rip the cloud from the frescoed sky,
Or tear the man from his place in the moon,
Fur from the buzzard and plumes from the coon,
But you can't tear me from the truth I cry,
That life is loathsome and love a lie.
She lifted me up to her bare brown face,
She cracked my ribs in her brown embrace,
And there in the shanty, side by side,
Each on the other's bosom died.

She's now the mistress of Buffalo Bill,
And pure as the heart of a lily still;
While I've killed all who have cared for me,
And I'm just as lonely as I can be,
So, pass the whiskey, — we'll have a spree!

OMNES. The real thing!

ZOÏLUS. You've beaten us all, but no wonder! Much of Joaquin Miller's verse is itself a travesty of poetry. Ancient, you talk about high ideals of literary art, and all that sort of thing: can you tell me what Rossetti and the rest of the English critics mean, in hailing this man as the great American poet?

THE ANCIENT. One thing, of course, they cannot see, — the thorough spuriousness of his characters, with their costumes, scenery, and all other accessories. Why, he takes Lara and the Giaour, puts them in a fantastic, impossible country called "Arizona" or "California," and describes them with a rhythm borrowed from Swinburne and a frenzy all his own, — and we are called upon to accept this as something original and grand! The amazed admiration of a class in England, and the gushing gratitude of one in America, form, together, a spectacle over which the pure, serene gods must bend in convulsions of inextinguishable laughter.

Zoïlus. Give me your hand! As Thackeray said, let us swear eternal friendship! You have often provoked me by persistently mollifying my judgments of authors; but, if you had done so in this case, I could not have forgiven you. Joaquin Miller, and he alone, would prove the decadence of our literature: he is an Indianized copy of Byron, made up of shrieks and war-paint, and the life he describes is too brutal, selfish, and insane ever to have existed anywhere. A few fine lines or couplets, or an occasional glittering bit of description, are not enough to make him a genius, or even an unusual talent.

The Gannet. But the material — not *his*, the true, Arizonian material — is good, and he has shown shrewdness in selecting it. He is clever, in some ways, or he never could have made so much capital in England. His temporary success here is only an echo of his success there.

Zoïlus. If he were a young fellow of twenty, I should say, wait; but his is not the exaggeration of youth, it is the affectation of manhood.

Galahad. If anybody ever seriously said, "Alas!" I should say it now. I have picked up many a grain of good counsel in the midst of our fun, and the fun itself has become an agreeable stimulus which I shall miss. We must not give up our habit wholly.

Zoïlus. There is no end of intellectual and poetic gymnastics, which we may try. I propose that we close with a grand satirical American "Walpurgis-Night," modelled on Goethe's Intermezzo in *Faust*.

THE GANNET. That is a good idea, but how shall we carry it out?

ZOÏLUS. Let each write a stanza or two, satirizing some literary school, author, magazine, or newspaper, throw it into the hat, and then take another, as long as we can keep up the game. When all are exhausted, give the hat to the Ancient and let him read the whole collection of squibs, in the order in which they turn up.

OMNES (*eagerly*). Accepted!

[Here, I am compelled to state, my liberty as a reporter ceases. The plan was carried out, and I think it was not entirely unsuccessful. But our mirth was partly at the expense of others: many of the stanzas were only lively and good-humored, but many others thrust out a sharp sting in the last line. As I was not an accomplice, I was perfectly willing that they should all be given to the public. Zoïlus did not seriously object; but the other three were peremptory in their prohibition. Even the Gannet confessed that he was not courageous enough to run the risk of making half a dozen permanent enemies by shafts of four lines apiece: he knew how largely the element of *personal* profit and reputation enters into American literary life, and how touchy a sensitiveness it develops. There was no denying this, for they related many instances to prove it. I yielded, of course, although it was a disappointment to me. After having thus entered authorship by a side-door, as it were, I find the field very pleasant; and I withdraw now, since there is no alternative, with reluctance. — THE NAMELESS REPORTER.]

THE BATTLE OF THE BARDS.

[AT the opening of the Fair of the American Institute, in New York, on the 7th of September, 1871, an original poem of some length was recited by Walt Whitman. At that time Bret Harte's and Colonel John Hay's admirable dialect ballads were read by everybody, and the sudden popularity which Joaquin Miller had obtained in England, a few months previous, made him the subject of much newspaper remark. The fact that these four authors, notwithstanding the very different quality of their work, were then specially prominent in public interest, suggested travesties which should represent them as rivals, each claiming ascendency over the others. The greater part of Walt Whitman's production was published in the "New York Tribune" on the 8th of September, in the report of the opening of the Fair; and on the same day, the four following imitations, without the connecting prose passages, were sent to that paper. The latter were added by the editor then in charge, and probably contributed even more to the amusement of the public than the poems themselves. The rare liberality — nay, in a literary sense, generosity—which the editor exhibited would be universally appreciated, if it were proper to mention his name.]

E have never regretted so much as yesterday the limited capacity of our eight pages which compelled us to omit some portions of Mr. Whitman's remarkable poem. It was perhaps the most remarkable which has ever been delivered before an Industrial Assembly, and we are assured by the offi-

cers of the Signal Service that it is not probable that another such disturbance of the elements will take place this century. It is this consideration which induces us to print the following choice extract which was yesterday ransomed, at great expense, from the hands of the Celtic lady who sweeps out the office. The Night Editor has been severely censured for slaughtering this exquisite morceau, and compared to the base Judean who threw a pearl away richer than all his agate.

WALT WHITMAN.

Who was it sang of the procreant urge, recounted sextillions of subjects?
Who but myself, the Kosmos, yawping abroad, concerned not at all about either the effect or the answer;
Straddling the Continent, gathering into my hairy bosom the growths, whatever they were, and nothing slighted, nothing forgotten?
Allez! I am the One, the only One, and this is my Chant Democratique.
Where is he that heard not, and she that heard not, and they that heard not, before and during and after?
All is wholesome and clean, and all is the effluent strain, impeccable, sweet, of the clasper of comrades.
If there were anything else, I would sing it;
But there is nothing, no jot or tittle, or least little scraping of subject or matter:
No, there is nothing at all, and all of you know it.

[We make room for further portions of our report of the opening of the Institute, which were crowded out yesterday.]

When Mr. Whitman's voice had died away among the patent pumps and corn-cutters which cumbered the vast amphitheatre, a slight but elegantly formed gentleman lounged forward from among the refrigerators, and said in a voice of singular sweetness, —

"Air this a free fight?"

His face was the face of Raphael and his boots were the boots of Cinderella. His black curls fell damply over a high, pale brow, but were not materially injured by the fall. An enormous diamond, the dying gift of Pinky the Bilk, whom he had tenderly shot in church one day at Sandy Bar for being a half-second out of time on the Amens, glittered on his lady-like finger. By one of those cynical contrasts of the frontier, his garb was by Poole, but his mustache was dyed by Day and Martin.

"I've heerd," he continued, putting his hand behind his hip, "that this was a trial trip of song-sharps. Ef so, I'll jest chip in. I'm from Roaring Camp, near Skunk's Misery, and my name is — well, you know that, if you know anything." He read with exquisite expression the following: —

> Who? Well — comin' so suddent,
> I'm hardly ready to say.
> I know: but I'd rather you would n't
> Put it to me just that way.
> Not that my stripe is modest;
> That was rubbed off long ago:
> And I *have* been questioned the oddest
> And I'm not altogether slow.
>
> Come, — set up to this here table!
> You! — bring us two more beers!

Could n't I put it as a fable,
　　Sich as a boy often hears?
You know every gard'ner mulches
　　Round some partic'lar tree:
Men read, in the deepest gulches,
　　And so — they 've found out *me!*

'T was cuttin' a queer sort o' capers,
　　So the folks out there said;
But I ask you to look in the papers,
　　And see what stuff 's most read.
Why, Jim, the very way I met you
　　People knows, far and near, —
Knows from my tellin', — and yet you
　　Ask me who 's first! It 's queer.

Hang it! what 's the use o' beatin'
　　Round the bush in this here way?
And you doin' all the treatin',
　　And me with nothing to say!
Here 's to *us!* — this way I can show it,
　　If you have n't already guessed:
We 're drinkin' the health o' the poet
　　That 's flattened out all the rest!

Here a long, lank, farmer-looking man, with travel-stained garments of Kentucky jeans, a weather-beaten face, rough with two days of grizzled beard, enormous brown hands and wrists protruding from the short coat-sleeves, and a general air of melancholy and tobacco about him, came slouching up to the platform, and taking off his tattered fur cap, said to the President, —

"Good morning, Jedge! I drapped in to take a hand

'long o' the other poets, but ef ye ain't got no better stock nor this, I reckon I'll skeet back to Spunky Pint. Why, Jedge! my little Gabe — he's at school at Hell's Bend in Magoopin Co. — dogg on my skin ef he can't sing the socks off'n that thar little Gambolier."

"Confine yourself to your own poetry," said the chairman, austerely; and the Pike sadly shook the hay-seed from his long iron-gray hair, and read these rhymes, in a snuffling tone curiously at variance with their libertine tendency : —

    You fellows East may sing as you please,
        And tickle the scalps of all concerned ;
    You may cant away with Cantharides,
        Rip with Euripides, and be derned !
    But to find the real high-pressure style,
        And travel the stavingest road to glory,
    You must go out West for a thousand mile,
        And never stop till you pass Peory.

    We don't prance round in white kid gloves,
        Smellin' of grease and sassyfrack :
    Our vittles ain't honey and turtle-doves,
        And when *we* kiss, it's a reg'lar smack.
    We take things rough, but we swaller 'em whole ;
        We don't pretend to be simperin' pious ;
    And what we are fit for, blast my soul !
        If you want to know, come out and try us !

    These here United States, they say,
        Is owin' the world an outfit of verse:
    Pike County 'll fix it, any day,
        And who goes furder 'll fare the worse.

> There 's a man lives out on the peraira thar,
>   In an old shebang, as I 've heard tootin',
> And if hisn don't go through your hide and har,
>   It 's my opinion there 'll be some shootin'.

A wild war-whoop resounded through the building, and a wilder apparition burst upon the scene. He was dressed from head to foot in buckskin dyed a fiery red; strings of silver bells tinkled about him; his face was painted in broad alternate bands of green, yellow, and crimson; a long scalp-lock, stiffened with eagle's feathers, reached half-way to the ceiling. [Mr. Shanks ordered this report to be *strong*. I hope this will suit. — REPORTER.] In a voice loud enough to drown the whistle of ten locomotives, he read in a strange runic chant the following poem, from a manuscript signed JOAQUIN, written in letters of blood on the tanned hide of a Camanche princess : —

> Far on the hot Apache plain
> I sinched the girth and I buckled the rein :
> The glorious girl behind me sang,
> But I sprang to the saddle without a pang,
> And gave the spur to my wild mustang,
> And a coil of the loose riata's fold
> Over his flanks like a serpent rolled,
> As his hoofs went forward, and forward, and on,
> Till the plain, and the hills, and the girl, were gone.
> The forests of cactus stabbed and stung,
> The sun beat down on my skinless tongue,
> The dust was thick in my simmering mouth,
> And a whirlwind of flame came out of the South,
> From the dry bananas, whose fiery hair

Singed the monkeys and parroquets there.
I crashed through the flame, I dashed o'er the sand,
Bearing my songs in my red right hand,
Bearing the songs of the Western land,
Tender and glowing and fierce and grand.
Take them and read them and yield me the crown
Which the old Sierras on me cast down
From peaks untrodden, of gorgeous glare,
Cast down upon me and bade me wear!
And whoso denies it he shall be
Struck, and despised, and spit on, by me,
As a loathsome snake, as a venomous thing,
Fit but to swelter and crawl and sting,
And build his cell in the rotten, rank
Recess of a noisome toadstool bank,
While I, like a hawk in the splendid sky,
Scream revenge as I wheel on high,
And the sound of my screaming shall never die!

OBITUARY. — Ananias Longbow, of our City Department, yesterday fell or was thrown from the third-story windows of THE TRIBUNE building. No cause is assigned for the rash act.

A REVIEW.

[Published in the "New York Tribune," December 4, 1875.]

THE INN ALBUM. By Robert Browning. James R. Osgood & Co.

HAT's this? A book? 16mo. — Osgood's page,
   Fair, clear, Olympian-typed, and save a scant
     O' the margin, stiff i' the hurried binding,
     good!
Intituled how? "*The Inn Album, Robert Brown-
ing, Author.*" Why should he not say, as well,
The Hotel Register? — cis-Atlantic term!
Nay, an he should, the action might purvey
To lower comprehensions: so not he!
Reflect, 't is Browning! — he neglects, prepense,
All forms of form: what *he* gives must we take,
Sweet, bitter, sour, absinthean, adipose,
Conglomerate, jellied, potted, salt, or dried,
As the mood holds him; ours is not to choose!
Well (here huge sighs be heard!) commending us
To Heaven's high mercy, let us read!

       — Three hours:
The end is reached; but who begins review,
Forgetful o' beginning, with the end?
Turn back! — why, here's a line supplies us with
Curt comment on the whole, though travesty, —
Hail, calm obliquity, lugubrious plot! —
Yea, since obliquity the straight path is,
And Passion worships as her patron saint
The Holy Vitus, and from Language fall
The rusty chains of rhythm and harmony,
Why not exclaim, "*Hail, sham obliquity!*"
Too hard, you murmur, sweet submissive minds? —
But take a bite o' the original pie! Set teeth,
'Ware cherry-stones, and if a herring-spine
Stick crosswise i' the throat, go gulp, shed tears,
But blame not us! So runs the opening: —

 "That oblong book's the Album; hand it here!
  Exactly! page on page of gratitude
  For breakfast, dinner, supper, and the view!
  I praise these poets: they leave margin-space;
  Each stanza seems to gather skirts around,
  And primly, trimly, keep the foot's confine,
  Modest and maidlike; lubber prose o'ersprawls
  And straddling stops the path from left to right.
  Since I want space to do my cipher-work,
  Which poem spares a corner? What comes first?.
  '*Hail, calm acclivity, salubrious spot!*'
  (Open the window, we burn daylight, boy!)
  Or see — succincter beauty, brief and bold —
  '*If a fellow can dine On rump steaks and port wine
  He needs not despair Of dining well here* —'

' *Here!* ' I myself could find a better rhyme.
 That bard's a Browning; he neglects the form!
 But ah, the sense, ye gods, the weighty sense!"

This bard's a Browning! — there's no doubt of that:
But, ah, ye gods, *the sense!* Are we so sure
If sense be sense unto our common-sense,
Low sense to higher, high to low, no sense
All sense to those, all sense no sense to these?
That's where your poet tells! — and you've no right
(Insensate sense with sensuous thought being mixed)
To ask analysis! How can else review,
Save in the dialect of his verse, be writ?
So write we: (would we might foresee the end!)
So has he taught us, i' " The Ring and The Book,"
De gustibus, concerning taste, *non est*
There's no — disputing, *disputandum* (Ha!
'T is not so difficult) — and we submit.

Ring prompter's bell! — let to strange music rise.
The curtain: here's a country inn's best room;
The persons, two, have gambled all night through,
And now 't is morning. One's "a polished snob,"
Young, rich, yet with rough base of manliness
(We learn this afterward); the elder man,
A lord, the meanest scoundrel ever lived
(So we shall find), "refinement every inch
From brow to boot-end." Ciphers he in book, —
No paper else! — and, stead of snob's loss, finds
Himself the loser by ten thousand pounds!
Much dialogue ensues, — the substance this:
Snob offers to forgive the debt, keep mum;

With insult lord refuses, penniless
And overbearing. "*Father's apron still
Sticks out from son's court-vesture; still silk purse
Roughs finger with some bristle sow-ear born!*"
So speaketh he, "refinement every inch,"
Et cetera. Well, they pay the tavern bill,
Walk toward the station, lord intent to catch
The morning train to town, while snob remains
To seek a neighbor cousin, possible wife.
To ordinary persons here were end,
Not so to Browning-persons; wait a bit,
And you'll perceive the red-clawed Tragic's hawk
Pounce on the thoughtless chick of Commonplace,
I' midst o' dunghill-blessedness!

          As the two
Sighted the station, train unwhistled yet,
A gate invites: what fool such swinging seat,
Albeit sharp edge to gluteal want o' pad,
Disdaineth? Thereupon they perch, and then
Much dialogue ensues, — the upshot this:
Lord met, four years ago, admired, betrayed
A parson's daughter, tamely wedded now
And lost to him, — his chance of life no less
A loss: the apple ripe to hand withheld
Drops and the swine devour: he sees it now.
Snob met, four years ago, admired and loved,
And then renounced, the stateliest of her sex,
A lord befooled, then married, — so the tale:
Four years — a parson's daughter — was't the same?
Unmarried I, says lord; 't is not the same.

(But 't was the same of course: the reader sees
Cat's-whiskers where the meal is seeming smooth,
And tadpole-tails i' the mud;) so talking, train
Whisks past, no second till the afternoon,
And lord goes back to tavern, snob strides off
To visit aunt and cousin.
     Second scene:
(*Hail, calm obliquity, lugubrious plot!*)
Enter the cousin in the inn's best room,
With female friend, arrived by train! This friend —
"Superb one," Browning says, and we know whom! —
Summoned by cousin on the snob to hold,
Privately, judgment; should she wed or not?
Much dialogue ensues, — no substance now,
Mere beating round the bush, but one grows pale,
The other wonders, — reader, haply, thinks
The Devil's to pay when all together meet!

Superb one left alone, comes back my lord,
Seeing not first the lady watching elm
At window, takes the "Inn Album," opens page,
And (Heaven knows why!) reads once again:
"*Hail, calm acclivity, salubrious spot!*"
Thereat, explosions: with "black-blooded brow"
The lady fronts him, — hate, defiance, rage,
Burn, spit, hiss, boil, and bubble in her speech.
Then he, in turn, "refinement every inch
From brow to boot-end," answers thus: —

   "So, I it was allured you — only I —
   I, and none other — to this spectacle —

Your triumph, my despair — you woman fiend
That front me! Well, I have my wish, then! See
The low wide brow oppressed by sweeps of hair
Darker and darker as they coil and swathe
The crowned corpse-wanness whence the eyes burn black.
Not asleep now! not pin-points dwarfed beneath
Either great bridging eyebrow — poor blank beads —
Babies, I've pleased to pity in my time:
How they protrude and glow immense with hate!
The long triumphant nose attains — retains
Just the perfection; and there's scarlet-skein
My ancient enemy, her lip and lip,
Sense-free, sense-frighting lips clenched cold and bold
Because of chin, that based resolved beneath!
Then the columnar neck completes the whole
Greek-sculpture-baffling body! Do I see?
Can I observe? You wait next word to come?
Well, wait and want! since no one blight I bid
Consume one least perfection. Each and all,
As they are rightly shocking now to me,
So may they still continue! Value them?
Ay, as the vender knows the money-worth
Of his Greek statue, fools aspire to buy,
And he to see the back of! Let us laugh!
You have absolved me from my sin at least!
You stand stout, strong, in the rude health of hate,
No touch of the tame timid nullity
My cowardice, forsooth, has practised on!
Ay, while you seemed to hint some fine fifth act
Of tragedy should freeze blood, end the farce,
I never doubted all was joke. I kept,
May be, an eye alert on paragraphs,
Newspaper notice — let no inquest slip,

>   Accident, disappearance: sound and safe
>   Were you, my victim, not of mind to die!"

Answer to this brutality (when we
Think who and what the two, abominable!)
Vouchsafes she, — story of her wedded life,
Husband a country curate, stupidly
Yet most devoutly saving stupid souls,
Whose interests she, this goddess in the flesh,
Endures in ennui killing heart and brain,
Life grown a hell, save for defiant pride
To answer *him*, — yea, wild, illogical,
She moves us somewhat. Hearken now to him,
Who thus speaks, after insult: —

>   "God forgives;
>   Forgive you, delegate of God, brought near
>   As never priest could bring him to this soul
>   That prays you both — forgive me! I abase —
>   Know myself mad and monstrous utterly
>   In all I did that moment; but as God
>   Gives me this knowledge — heart to feel and tongue
>   To testify — so be you gracious too!
>   Judge no man by the solitary work
>   Of — well, they do say and I can believe —
>   The devil in him: his, the moment, — mine
>   The life — your life!

>   He names her name again.
>   You were just — merciful as just, you were
>   In giving me no respite: punishment
>   Followed offending. Sane and sound once more,
>   The patient thanks decision, promptitude,
>   Which flung him prone and fastened him from hurt

Haply to others, surely to himself.
I wake and would not you had spared one pang.
All 's well that ends well! "

And so on, for the space of ninety lines,
The brute and blackguard mouths his lyric love,
Falls on his knees, abases to the dust
His haughty selfishness. To which relapse
This much (much else omitted) is the pith
Of her reply : —
" You are the Adversary!
Your fate is of your choosing: have your choice!
Wander the world, — God has some end to serve,
Ere he suppress you! He waits: I endure,
But interpose no finger-tip, forsooth,
To stop your passage to the pit. Enough
That I am stable, uninvolved by you
In the rush downward: free I gaze and fixed;
Your smiles, your tears, prayers, curses move alike
My crowned contempt. You kneel? Prostrate yourself
To earth, and would the whole world saw you there!"

A step: a voice "*All right!*" outside; the snob
Comes back a-sudden, pushes wide the door,
Sees kneeler, kneeled-to, deeply breathes an "Ah-h!"
— True melodrama! *Take this pur-r-rse of gold,
Me hated rival: in another l-l-land
'T will make thee r-r-rich!* You 're wrong, my eager
    f-f-friend,
Dead out o' reckoning! What says the snob,
Whom scattered evidence of manliness
Made seem a man? No explanation sought,

He belches bile and gall, stirs gutter-filth,
Names "bag and baggage," "friend-and-goddess love,"
Insults, bespatters, rages. She, between,
Soothes him, defies the other; then this last,
His knees still dusty from the abject prayer,
Again is devil. (Hark ye, here 's the dodge
To cook original passion : what men do
Don't let them do, and what they never do
Do : none can guess what next shall hap i' the tale;
Passion is incoherent, and you 've still
Nature to fall upon.) This Album-book —
Hail, sham obliquity, lugubrious plot!
Is wellnigh read; you end the tangle, smash!
Here 's Browning's recipe; take heaps o' hate,
Take boundless love, hydraulic-pressed, in bales,
Distilments keen of baseness and of pride,
And innocence and cunning, — mix 'em well,
And put a body round 'em! Add the more
O' this, or that, you have another, — stay!
The sex don't count; make female of the male,
Male female, all the better; let them meet,
Talk, love, hate, cross, till satisfied — then, kill!
So here : lord, finding situation tough
(Between two fires, hate and a horsewhip-threat),
Writes i' the Album, goes without and waits.
Superb One, having read, takes hand of snob,
Accepts his love till death; then lord comes back.
What did he write? "Refinement every inch
From brow to boot-end," 't was a threat to tell
The country curate of his wife's disgrace, —
He, the disgracer! Snob gets wild at that,
Screams, jumps, and clutches. . . . .

All at once we see
One character dead — but how, we don't quite know.
Then she, Superb One, writes in Album, dies
By force of will, (no hint of instrument!)
Leaving the snob alone and much surprised.
Cousin is heard without; but ere the door
Opens, the story closes. Only this remains,
The last conundrum, hardly guessable
By the unbrowninged mind. Since what it means,
If aught the meaning, means some other thing
And that thing something else, but this not that,
Nor that the other, — we adopt the lines
As most expressing what we fail express,
Our solemn verdict, handkerchief and all,
Upon the book: we quote, with grateful heart: —

> "All's ended and all's over! Verdict found
> '*Not guilty*' — prisoner forthwith set free,
> Mid cheers the Court pretends to disregard!
> Now Portia, now for Daniel, late severe,
> At last appeased, benignant! '*This young man —*
> *Hem — has the young man's foibles but no fault,*
> *He's virgin soil — a friend must cultivate.*
> *I think no plant called " love " grows wild — a friend*
> *May introduce, and name the bloom, the fruit !*'
> Here somebody dares wave a handkerchief —
> She'll want to hide her face with presently!
> Good by then! '*Cigno fedel, cigno fedel,*
> *Addio !*' Now, was ever such mistake —
> Ever such foolish ugly omen? Pshaw!
> Wagner beside! '*Amo te solo, te*
> *Solo amai !*' That's worth fifty such!
> But, mum, the grave face at the open door!"

The meaning ask you, O ingenuous soul?
Why, were there such for you, what then were left
To puzzle brain with, pump conjecture dry,
And prove you little where the poet's great?
Great must he be, you therefore little: — go!
The curtain falls, the candles are snuffed out:
End, damned obliquity, lugubrious plot!

PARADISE DISCOVERED.

AN EPIC.

OF Pork and Beans, which from the primal East,
Beyond the Indian Mount, where early tricks
Her purfled scarf old Tithon's paramour,
And Arimaspean giants, famed of old,
Ravaged the Scythian plains, the nations bore
Westward to Celtic and the Saxon fields,
And thence o'er dangers of the glistering seas
To bloom, transplanted, on New England soil,
I sing: and thou, who givest ample food
To palates sated with Parisian feasts,
Apician god, whether thy feet be stayed
In markets vast, beside the minted lamb,
Or from the fumes of savory coppers tak'st
Delight of boiling beef, commend my song,
And raise it to that height of argument
Which makes the theme, full humble though it be,
Grander than strains of old Mæonides.
For I upon that famous dish was nurst,
Scoffed at erewhile, whose now acknowledged worth
The round world echoes, — whence increase of use,

And pæans louder than the orby clang
Of shields at Radamont or Mandragore,
Or where Biscayan bulwarks front the wave
Trebonian, or of Syrtis by Cyrene
Borasmian thunders : nor no lesser joy,
Though silent, cheek distent with pungent weed,
Feel Siasconset's fishers, homeward blown
From broad Hyannis and the shoaling sands,
When all the air, from every chimney-flue,
Breathes odors of the Dish ; and each his own
With practised nostril from the steamy twine
Untangles. Hail! thou bright, warm effluence!
Hail, wedded nourishment! —

(*Cetera desunt*, owing to the precipitate flight of the indignant Muse.)

www.ingramcontent.com/pod-product-compliance
Lightning Source LLC
Chambersburg PA
CBHW020245170426
43202CB00008B/236